SPOTLIGHT
ON THE
ART OF GRACE

Edited by: Christine Jones

Contributors:

Mark Fegan ▪ Rebecca Fegan ▪ Gloria Harmon
George Hast ▪ Christine Jones ▪ Keith Jones
Chip Mackenzie ▪ Evelyn Mosley ▪ Nick Wolff

Copyright © 2016 by The Alternative Book Club

Edited by Christine L. Jones

Cover Design by Nick Wolff

Alternativebookclub.com

Published in association with Keith Jones of Kitewind, LLC.

Printed and bound in the United States of America.

First Edition

ISBN 978-1-365-40455-9

All rights reserved. No part of the material protected by this copyright notice may be reproduced or utilized in any form or by any means, electronic or mechanical, including photocopying, recording or by any information storage or retrieval system without the written permission of the copyright owner.

Spotlight on the Art of Grace

Contents

BEFORE YOU START i

DEDICATION iv

BRINGING GOOD ENERGY 1
By: Rebecca Fegan

THE ART OF THE APOLOGY 27
By: Nick Wolff

TAKE NO OFFENSE 57
By: Gloria Harmon

LEADING FROM BEHIND 81
By: Evelyn Mosley

GRACE AND HUMOR 95
By: George Hast

GRACE IN THE WORKPLACE 113
By: Keith Jones

THANKFULNESS 139
By: Charles W. "Chip" Mackenzie, Ph. D.

BREAKING THE MOLD 161
By: Christine Jones

TURNING LIFE EXPERIENCES INTO LEARNING EXPERIENCES 183
By: Mark Fegan

BIOGRAPHIES 211

Before you start...

As with most good things in life, we appreciate the moment more when we have full understanding of how we arrived here together. This group of dedicated people began with a few who wanted to gain more than we were getting from a club to which we all belong. We agreed that we needed different tools than what were available to us. We began to meet together socially to "pick each other's brains" as to how to achieve our dreams. These brainstorming sessions have helped us get to know each other along with our goals and needs. Some want to write while some want to become professional speakers. Some in the group have experience doing these things and are willing to share this knowledge with others. The others liked the idea of gaining experience by working together on an actual project.

Since we are not a typical book club, we began to call ourselves The Alternative Book Club. Typical clubs meet to study a book. We meet to write a book. Every one has worked to support each other and make this happen.

During our chats, it became very evident that this group of diverse people has a common thread of experience. Grace. Just looking through dictionary.com or Webster Dictionary, you will find many definitions. "A virtue." "A controlled polite, and pleasant way of behaving." "Goodwill." "Be so kind." These are just a few. We have each already had experiences where grace has been a factor of our getting through them. Everyone is willing to share our stories with you. Through them you will see how grace was a factor.

We all agree that a classic example of the lack of grace occurs when a toddler has a temper tantrum. They are frustrated and unable to communicate, which leads them into a fit of rage. Adults can be reduced to their own tantrum as they try to resolve their toddler's issues. Our hope is that this book will give you realistic examples to help you avoid having any future tantrums by showing you how using grace is a better approach.

That is how the thought of collaborating on a book came into being our goal. We are getting an opportunity to learn and practice new skills while creating a new tool toward our common goal of helping others. You will notice, each Chapter has been written by a different person. Hence, you will see how grace can get you through life from several perspectives.

In order for you to gain the most from this book, we suggest that you prepare to make notes as you reflect how grace affects you. Each Chapter will provide you opportunities to stop and think. Our desire is for this book to be used by individuals as well as be appropriate for a study group or a typical book club. We welcome you and thank you for spending your time with our group!

We have sought to eliminate all typos so as not to distract you from our messages. We humbly ask you to gracefully forgive us for any mistakes that we may have overlooked in the making of this book.

Mainly, we hope that our lessons of grace will help you find the moments of grace in your life.

Dedication

This book would not have been possible without the graceful dedication of everyone involved in The Alternative Book Club. To each, I need to say a heartfelt, "Thank YOU!"

We each have dedications that we would like to see printed here. Rather than add another chapter, I will ask you to give thought to the families from which we came. Many other people have touched our lives through thought, word, and deed. We are thankful to each one. We dedicate this to all of you.

The quotes at the beginning of each chapter are inspirational to us. May they also be inspiring to you.

This entire book is dedicated to those who have given us grace. Through you we have gained knowledge and are able to give grace to others.

May you, the reader, find and give grace, too.

On behalf of the entire group,
Christine Jones, Editor

1

Bringing Good Energy

By: Rebecca Fegan

"When you show deep empathy toward others, their defensive energy goes down, and positive energy replaces it. That's when you can get more creative in solving problems."

~Stephen Covey

Introduction

Let me introduce myself. I have been called the Energizer Bunny. As a member of Toastmasters since 2008, I have belonged to 4 clubs in various positions such as Secretary, who as you know, completely controls everything in a Toastmaster club from minutes to running of meetings and acting as the memory of the group, or Treasurer, which, as you can imagine, controls everything in a Toastmaster club from collecting dues to determining the activities and influencing the growth of the club, or VP of Membership, who you would assume would be the driving force behind any club's growth and the growth of the members... you see? Apparently it doesn't matter what position I take, the club believes that the Bunny brings the Charge! I have worked at a myriad of jobs ranging from teaching music for 50 years to substitute teaching to being a stockbroker. The examples I use in this chapter are mostly taken from my time in fast food where I spent (invested?) 10 years of my life. I firmly believe that the attitude of the people you work with depends on how well they connect to each other, and that anyone can affect the morale of the group and the energy of the group by likewise connecting to those around them. We do that by bringing good energy to a group.

<u>Grace in a Group by Bringing Good Energy</u>

That's an intriguing prospect isn't it! How do you get people in your club, your team, your workplace, or your family to an interactive, positive place full of enthusiasm and good will? Is this the natural state of things? I think, if you look around your environment, you'll discover it is easier to be cynical, self-centered, grouchy, or depressed. However, if you are familiar with professional sports events, you know that the "6th man" syndrome in basketball or all the fans in the crowd in <u>any</u> sport cheering and bringing energy to the team is a major factor in the energy of the team. Even in teams that don't win regularly, there's a palpable feeling among the fans that this is THEIR team and they will support it as many times as they play. Brad Simpson writes of the Cubs fans in his blog, "Cubs fans of course understand what it is like to live with pain and diabolical disappointment...we understand what it means (as I swear I once heard Billy Corgan say on the radio), to have a sliver of hope in which we will eventually hang ourselves." Yet, people carry their love of the team like a badge of honor. You'll also run across a team that wins regularly, but the fans will be cynical and hypercritical. Look at the UNL Huskers. After Tom Osborne left his coaching position. Frank Solich replaced him. Coach Solich had been working with the Huskers while an assistant to Tom Osborne, so he was familiar with the way they played and the members of his team. But when they didn't win <u>all</u> of their games, the fans DEMANDED his head. During the games, they all cheered and were supportive, but in between games, they sliced the coach to ribbons. The secret is the **energy** brought to the table, and it applies to every situation, not just sports.

There are several things that you have to bring to the table to get this positive energy. First of all, you have to have your own positive energy. It's an attitude, an approach to life in all types of circumstances that gives people a sense that everything will be all right. It's the projection that you will win, that you will have fun doing what it takes to win, and there will be nothing to stop you. I knew a college teacher, Dr. Bill, who had this kind of energy. He taught an economics course among other business classes. Economics, both macro and micro, is dreaded universally by every business major with very few exceptions. You could tell by his face that Dr. Bill LOVED the subject and was anxious to spread this love to his students so they could appreciate the subject as much as he did. When he taught the concepts, it was as if he had just discovered them that morning and HAD to share what he found with us before he burst with excitement. He always had a smile on his face. He taught by asking us questions that would lead us to discover these concepts for ourselves and was ecstatic when the light bulbs came on in our brains. His positive energy brought the subject and the students to life. His approach to the students in his class showed grace—he genuinely cared if people learned and applied the material he taught.

Here is a story of how good energy brought to a bad situation can turn it around. I knew a fast food manager working with a small crew who was faced with 2 charter buses full of football players and coaches that stopped at his restaurant near closing time. As things rapidly deteriorated and the crew was overwhelmed, he called one of his best back-liners to come and help, and as she lived just across the street, she quickly came to his rescue. When she arrived, the back line was a disaster! There was lettuce ankle deep on the floor, they were out of ¼ pound burgers and condiments, and all of the football players were ordering the buy one get one special ¼ pounders. The cooks were in a panic and yelling at each other. She calmly walked in and told the secondary sandwich maker to grab a broom and start sweeping up. He was confused, but he did it. Then she assigned one person to just fry up ¼ pound burgers until she told him to stop, and another to drop fries (cook them--not drop them on the floor!) until she told him to stop. She had the secondary sandwich maker refill the condiment table after he finished sweeping. As soon as the first set of ¼ pounders came off the grill, she zipped into action, and she and the primary sandwich maker started making the specials and the small burgers. They made 100 ¼ pound specials, 20 of the various other sandwiches (chicken, bacon cheeseburgers, and mushroom/Swiss) and about 30 of the junior sized burgers in less than 15 min. The whole time they were kidding around, laughing, and joking, and this back-liner inspired hope and brought the energy level up to a place that the night crew had never experienced before. She diffused the panic and replaced it with Grace. To get a scope of what this took, the grill person was doing 3 runs of 10 ¼-pound burgers every 2 ½-min, 10 junior burgers every 5 min, and 5 grilled chicken every 7 min. The fry person did about 120 pounds of fries altogether with 3 fryers going down every 3 min. He also was doing 3, breaded chicken every 5 min. The sandwich makers were doing about 6-10 sandwiches a minute. The secondary sandwich maker was keeping things stocked and moving product to the stations. He was cleaning in between runs. When they finished the rush, the floors were clean, the surfaces wiped, the back line freezers were stocked, the grill was scraped and polished, and you wouldn't have known there had been any buses in that night. No one was yelling or short-tempered. They were all high-fiving each other and patting each other on the back. This high energy produced synergy. They all knew that if this back-liner was there and she was not panicked, everything was going to turn out OK. Slowly, but surely, the energy of the rest of the crew started to build, and they got into a "zone" where everything just fell into place. She brought her good energy to the situation, and she knew how to approach the situation with grace and keep the morale up.

As you can see, you must bring your own good energy into a situation to spark the energy of the others on the team. Getting your own good energy is the subject of another study, but you have to HAVE good energy to BRING good energy.

Assessing the Current Energy of Your Group

Get out your notebook. You need to write down your observations.

Look at your current situation. What kind of energy do you see? What kinds of attitudes are most prevalent? Do your people interact? Do your managers communicate with the employees and with the upper management? What kind of environment do you see? Are there motivational/inspirational posters everywhere? Are there awards? How punctual are people when they come to your location? If they seem to drag in with coffee in hand and leave as soon as the second hand indicates the end of the shift, you may have an energy problem. Do you sense tension when the boss comes in? Do you see furtive looks on the employees? Are there raised voices, complaints, or, little niggling notes on the bulletin board? What kind of language do you observe? Is it mostly verbal (notes, complaints, insults, praise, or bragging)? Or do they use nonverbal communication as well (practical jokes, booby traps, hugs, high 5's, or favors)?

Some people communicate positively or negatively with words, "Hey, thanks for stocking me up! We had a real rush this morning!" or "You left me without any toner again! You jerk!" Some communicate with actions. John cleans up the break room kitchen before he leaves; or the night crew has a food fight the night before the District manager comes for an inspection. Some use a combination of words and actions when they communicate. Barry patronizes Susan, takes credit for her innovations and then promotes Wally over her. The day crew leaves really nasty notes for the night crew and complains to the General Manager all morning, and then they refuse to stock the night crew before they leave. Bill finds something to compliment his crew on every day and then awards an 'atta-boy' prize at the end of the week.

Look at the expressions on your team members' faces. Watch how they greet each other. Do they gossip, or do they concentrate on the task at hand? Do celebrations seem forced? Believe it or not, the opposite of good energy is not bad energy - it's LACK of energy - inertia as it were. It is much easier to move from bad energy to good than from NO energy to any type of energy. In any case, you must determine what kind of energy and at what level you have in your group. "On a scale of 1-5, my group energy is a positive 1." This means your group energy is generally positive, but not infectious, not impactful, and certainly not motivating. If it is negative and 5, you have broken pottery and holes in the walls. If it is 0, neither positive nor negative, you have an office of zombies.

Analyze the types of energy drains you have. Is it 1 department? 1 manager? 1 person? Do you sense resentment? Hopelessness? Are there too many distractions? Not enough reward for the perceived work put in? Boredom? Is there too much pressure? Are people assuming positions of responsibility without the requisite training and experience?

When you bring good energy to a group, you must make use of both types of languages—physical and verbal language. It's like the love language you use on your friends, your spouse or your children. If you see something that needs to be done, and you can do it, then do it. If you see that Sue is having a bad day, find out what could make her day better and do something special for her. Sometimes, it is as simple as saying something nice, but that means something nice about what she does well. "Sue, you really type fast! I'm amazed at your accuracy!" Or "Sue, your biscuits are so perfect, it's almost a crime to eat them!" Maybe she needs to get something done and doesn't have the time to do some of the little things. George needs her to get 20 copies made, and she needs to get the report finished for Bob. Offer to do the 20 copies. Is she low on paper? Is she low on toner or printer ink? Is her wastebasket full? See? Something as simple as a little physical help can make her feel valued and allow her to persevere to the end of her shift with just enough energy that she can pass it on to others. It affords a bit of grace in a particularly stressful situation that releases the tension and brings relief.

For another example: Fred has gotten slammed over the past week and is behind in his paperwork. As a manager, can you delegate someone to cover for Fred on the next case so he can get caught up? Marilyn has been working overtime to get the end of the year bonus, and she's really close. Can you throw some business her way so she can reach it? Can you offer to team up to get the jobs done more quickly so she can go on to the next client? What do these little acts of kindness do? They show the people you work with that they are valued. They raise the level of expectation among the people in the group… "Maybe we CAN make this goal!" It is a personal touch in an impersonal environment and it has a grand effect. In order for any of this to happen, and with good effect, you must be observant. You need to understand the environment as a whole, who or what is dragging down the energy, and understand each individual in your group—what they want, what they need, what they aspire to, what lights their fires.

If you understand the circumstances, you can start making inroads into improving the energy of the group. If a person or a group has complaints and they express them through verbal communication, the proper response is through action. The same goes for those complaints expressed by action: they must be addressed by verbal communication.

<u>Using the Correct Language to Address Concerns</u>

I was in a situation where the energy was bad. (I often find myself in these situations!) It was one of those "night crew vs. day crew" wars. Generally, in businesses that have a night crew and a day crew, the night crew consists of young, inexperienced, impulsive individuals. The day crew is made up of older, more experienced more mature people because they get First choice when it comes to shifts. When I got to this job, there was a ritual in place. The day crew arrived about 5:00 AM and spent the first 20-30 min. of each day cleaning up the mess left by the night crew in addition to getting their stations set up for opening. The General Manager would arrive about 10:00 AM to a crew of disgruntled, whining, grumbling, and complaining people. He would listen to their complaints for about 4 hours. The day crew would then leave scathing notes and insults for the night crew on the bulletin board. Notes with an individual's name were particularly unpleasant.

The night crew would arrive about 3:00 PM and work until an hour or so after close, which was about 11:00 PM. *The first thing they could look forward to every night was getting bawled out by the manager who had a list of everything the night crew had done wrong, and a slew of nasty notes on the bulletin board.* Instead of getting ready for their shifts however, they had to clean the machines, and do the prep work for the next day. At that point, with about 30 min. before the busiest time of the evening, they had to completely restock and be ready when the trickle of customers became a flood. They never left notes, though they complained to the manager that the day crew never got things ready for the night crew and they only had a half hour to get ramped up for the rush. They started out every night shift with bad attitudes and no inspiration to do a good job, so they made the shift bearable by playing games and goofing off. Then they got back at the day crew by sometimes booby trapping their stations, by emptying all the back line refrigerators and freezers so the day crew would have nothing to start with, and by hiding particularly smelly things (that tended to get Smellier!) in very hard to reach locations around the store.

As you can see, the verbal communication was met with action, which in turn, was met with more verbal communication. The energy was going bad very rapidly, and retaliation was escalating. It was very hard to hire and keep night crew. Turnover was nearly 4 times what it was on day crew. Some of the assistant managers and supervisors threatened to quit. Some of the day crew threatened to quit. The store was being

BRINGING GOOD ENERGY

threatened by the Health Department. The District Manager kept making unannounced visits (but only during the day, so he/she didn't <u>see</u> what was happening at night, he/she had to go by what they heard from the day crew and the other managers.) How do you turn around a situation like that? What would be the First thing you'd do? Add this to your notebook.

This is a chicken-egg situation. There are very few times when this is NOT the case. If there's negative energy, or no energy, you will find that it is cyclical. Nasty words—whether written or spoken will influence nasty actions and the effects escalate into full-blown wars. Do you think that if left unattended or unaddressed this store would survive? It is likely that eventually the General managers and the assistant managers would throw up their hands in the matter, and either lose some key individuals on both day and night crew, or quit themselves. Then the store's spiral would have no brakes and would crash and burn. In this particular store, this did indeed happen, but thanks to a shift supervisor it was five years later than it would have happened given its current trajectory. She got the trust of the night crew by coming in to help out when they needed it, and by getting along with the "kids" as they were called. This is where she showed Grace under pressure. She recommended some of the night crew be used for day crew on the weekends with her so they could see how day crew worked and what they

SPOTLIGHT ON THE ART OF GRACE

did. Then she trained one of the grill men, Shawn, how to properly clean the grill. A couple of days later, after Shawn had closed and cleaned the grill, she left him a note. Now remember that notes with names were particularly nasty, so when he saw it, he tossed it without reading it. She got into his face and made him take it out of the trash and read it. He was mad, but he complied. It said, "Shawn, you did a fantastic job on the grill! Remember that you sign your name to everything you do, and I recognized your grill this morning. My eggs slid across the grill! It was great! I stocked up your freezer for you." Shawn turned the note over to see the "but" and there wasn't one. He was very confused. He went to check the freezer and it was stuffed to the top. She asked him if he could train some of the other closers as to how to clean the grill. He said he would. Then he re-posted the note on the bulletin board for all to see. The next day, not only was the grill cleaned, but the stations were all stocked and there were no booby traps. **Our first rule then is:** make the communication you send (verbal or written) positive, and no "buts" allowed.

A few days later, Mike went to Susan (who was 50 years older than he) and asked her to train him how to make biscuits. Generally, everyone had to learn how to make biscuits by watching a video and then doing them according to the instructions until they could get "certified" and that was the end of it. Mike had been encouraged by this supervisor to get some advanced training. Mike and Susan DID NOT GET ALONG. He was told to cooperate, ask lots of questions and smile a lot. Susan was surprised by his request, and very suspicious. Mike got an ear full of nasty comments and snide remarks, but much to his credit, he made them into jokes and kept his temper. When Susan saw he was serious about learning the tricks of her trade, she taught him. He got to be much better, and as a result, the weekend biscuits were nearly the same quality as the weekday biscuits. He helped her clean up, and both of them got the station ready for each other. They became our Odd Couple. The notes regarding nasty things about Mike stopped completely and the back line morale went up. **Rule #2:** keep the communication open, and nip things in the bud by using both action and verbal communication. The encouragement of the supervisor was in the form of a note to Susan, which said, "I don't know what you did to Mike, but you must have performed some sort of hypnosis on him. His biscuits were amazing this morning! I had to double check to see who was baking! Thanks so much for helping him out!!!" All during Mike's shift (when he came into night crew) was peppered with "tatadaaaaahhhh! It's BISCUIT MAN! All hail to the god of biscuits!" He dutifully sprinkled his acolytes with the magic flour, and then cleaned furiously so Susan wouldn't be disappointed in him.

Now, it was hard for the day crew to say, "the NIGHT crew didn't do this or didn't do that" because they had to leave out Mike and Shawn's names. They couldn't make the generalities anymore. It was the same with the night crew. The day crew had gotten the moniker: Battle Axe Brigade. The night crew had to be more specific in their references to leave out the supervisor and Susan now. Neither group could say of the other, "They ALWAYS" or "They NEVER" because they sometimes got everything right. The character of the notes changed. Now instead of complaining about the state of the store and the fact that something really smelled awful somewhere in the vicinity of the salad supplies, the day crew was informing the night crew that the Health Inspection was Tuesday, and they completely stocked the night crew. Would the night crew PLEASE do an extra thorough job of cleaning? The night crew was informing the day crew that they were expecting a tour bus with 50 people about 5:30 and could they make some extra salads for the little old blue-haired ladies that would be in the tour? **Rule #3:** avoid generalities and lumping everyone into a group. The words "always" and "never" should be used in a positive way. "I love it when you close Chris; you <u>always</u> leave the equipment gleaming!" "I'm glad you <u>never</u> miss a corner when you sweep, Marla, because trying to use a car scraper to get the gunk that's been building up with the grease and the dust and the flour is like trying to chip cement. Thanks!" This makes the person you're complementing to not only continue in this helpful behavior, but to do it even better. It adds a touch of Grace to the communication and softens responses and encourages people to cooperate.

The escalation of camaraderie is noticeable. The escalation of nastiness and practical jokes and bad feelings is also noticeable. Which would you rather have? If you experience some good energy from your crew or your team or group, you should play on that. Catch them doing good things. Offer them compliments, help them out when they're in a bind, and be courteous. Show some grace. The result of this troubled store—turnover was reduced to 400%, which was the lowest in the district. Complaints were down to 1-2 a month instead of 14-16 per week. Average service speed—from time of order to receipt of order was among the fastest of the district and the health inspector would EAT THERE instead of bringing his own lunch like he had been doing.

If you sense some bad energy, isolate the cause then do something about it. Do not add to it by sending your own nasty notes or gossiping or getting retaliation. This same supervisor found that her efforts in the store under a *different manager* were going unappreciated. The main drain on the energy of the entire crew was the General Manager. He never came in early and often left to do personal errands. He had nothing but criticism for his crew and made no bones about their incapability, laziness, and stupidity to his District manager, and within earshot of some of the crew. He was inattentive of the details concerning the people he hired and scheduled. He once scheduled 16 year-olds to close and work on the grill, fryer and slicer, and the state rules are quite clear that people under 18 were not to engage in any of those things!

He ignored recommendations from his assistant managers. He ignored requests for days off and changes of shift. If a manager was in trouble—no crew, no supervisor, short on product, or dealing with gun-toting customers and he wasn't there, he'd reply to these pleas for help with, "It's my day to spend with my family. You're a manager, manage." And then he would hang up. The supervisor who had turned around the energy problems at the other store did a rage quit in this one. She left a 3-page letter on all the things that had gone wrong, especially those that were caused by his mismanagement, and pinned her keys to the bulletin board in the office and didn't show up again.

When the district manager called to beg her to come back, she read him a copy of her letter to the manager, and added details. What did this general manager do? He blamed the people he assigned to cover shifts, and he blamed the night crew for not setting things up (he was working night shift that night and made no attempt to prepare the store for the next day's special orders.) He called the supervisor a whiney crybaby that couldn't handle the simplest of problems. He took no blame on himself, and was completely surprised when the District manager confronted him about it. And yet, this manager was not fired; he was still working that same store a year later. In doing the things he did, he *escalated* the malaise that infected his store. The turnover rate went through the roof, complaints doubled, service times were rarely within the recommended range, and it was nearly impossible to keep an assistant or co-manager for more than 6-8 weeks, and they came very close to failing the health inspections. This is very important: **Rule #5:** be careful what you escalate!

The best thing you can do to make your energy positive, and that of your team is to approach everything with an attitude of gratitude. Yes, it is a cliché. It wouldn't be a cliché if it weren't a widespread solution. Instead of saying, "Every house in the neighborhood is without power, we have ½ a crew and we need to repair all the electric lines on the east side of

SPOTLIGHT ON THE ART OF GRACE

town!" we say, "Thank goodness that we have 15 people that made it in today, and with this crew of very good and dedicated workers, even though it is a long arduous task, we will be able to get it done in a more reasonable amount of time." Do you see the change in perspective? It gives the crew the attitude that they are part of an elite super hero team that can do things no one else could. Does that bring up the energy? YES!

Try to translate these sentences into statements of gratitude in your notebook.

1. There's a tornado coming and our principal is out of town! No one knows what to do with the students!
2. I have a report due on Friday, and since I was on vacation when I was told to submit it electronically, I only have my PDA—and there's no service here so I can't send it!
3. We have an ice cream social on Saturday, and we don't have anyone signed up to bring ice cream!

It's difficult isn't it! It takes determination and a paradigm shift to see problems as blessings we can use to grow, to learn something new, and to add energy rather than subtract it. Imagine the energy drain you'd have if in answer to #1 you said, "Well kiddoes and faculty, we're gonna die today. Put your head between your knees and kiss your butt goodbye." Or for #2, "Honey, do you have the want ads? Looks like I'm going to get fired because my Neanderthal of a boss wants me to submit a report and he KNEW I was on vacation without the information I needed to write the report and no access to a computer to send it." How about #3? "Well, if there's no ice cream, I'm not going to this. I know I organized it, but if they don't care, I'm not going to beat myself up about it. We'll just stay home and watch fireworks on TV." These statements would <u>definitely</u> pull energy from the people and the project wouldn't they! It takes effort and dedication and determination to keep your personal energy up. Let's look at the first situation: There's a tornado coming and the principal's out of town. "Hey Kids! Let's go see how many we can fit into the bathrooms! But they have to be on the first floor. Big kids, grab 3 little kids and make them part of your team. Little kids can get into wee bitty places. Now repeat after me, 'Auntie Em! Auntie Em! I can see my house from here!'" It also takes observation and analysis to find ways to change the energy flow from negative or neutral to positive. It's a lot of work, which brings me to my final point: You cannot do this forever, and you cannot do it alone.

<u>Getting Disciples!</u>

The problem that can be seen in the story about the supervisor that turned around the energy of the store was that the store failed 5 years later because she wasn't there to sustain the effort. Getting good energy into a situation doesn't sustain it in the long run; it must be renewed on a regular basis. You have to either keep hiring people with good energy, or train them up. The assistant managers and the general manager always breathed a sigh of relief when this supervisor came in. They didn't develop or bring in any of their own energy. Toward the end of the supervisor's tenure, the general attitude of these leaders was positive, but as a reaction to what the supervisor did, not in and of themselves. They fell back to their default attitude and eventually, so did the rest of the employees there.

The work that the supervisor did in improving the morale and the energy at the second store went largely unrecognized, and the general manager took credit for any improvement in service times, cleanliness, and turn over rates. When the supervisor quit, anyone with any positive energy realized that it was a lost cause, and either quit trying or quit out right. As a leader, you have an obligation to get more and more people to bring their good energy into the workplace, or club, or organization.

You train and develop these people the same way you bring good energy to your group—by using verbal and nonverbal communication. Reward and recognize their efforts to bring good energy. As a member of the crew, you do the same thing.

Energy can be passed up or passed down. The supervisor in the stories was an example of the trickle-up theory. If you ever read "Tearing Down the Walls" by Sandy Weill, you can see the trickle-down theory. Each of his sub managers had the same philosophy about business and nearly the same approach to keeping the energy up in their divisions. The results of both of these people, the supervisor and the CEO of Citigroup, were mind-blowing success. Turnover was reduced which brought down the cost of training new people as often, better efficiency, and advocated more team/family oriented relationships rather than adversarial and destructive relationships. This grace provided more positive energy and added secondary effects such as: more innovation, better client relationships, faster and bigger production, recognition, and basically adding value to the organization at every point.

One more story…

Summary

Dave was not an average guy. He grew up in a rural area, went to a 1-room school, and got average grades. He considered himself the black sheep of his family. He lucked into an opportunity by way of a relative that introduced him to the financial business. Dave was NOT financial business material. He didn't own a suit. He didn't have an MBA, and the only

SPOTLIGHT ON THE ART OF GRACE

thing he knew about loans was that he could never qualify for one. He studied and passed all his licenses and certifications, though, and was really excited about the prospects of helping his friends and his family and the members of his community with his new skills. He brought great energy to his office, and he attracted some others like him into the business. He was soon training and equipping these people to bring great energy to the business as well, and several branch managers were promoted out of his office—nine before he retired! He featured many of his team in his training sessions and treated them like rock stars. He taught them how to teach and how to present material to new people in the business. He praised them, he worked with them, and he jumped in when he was needed. He always kept his sense of humor and his people knew deep down that he believed in them. Because of this, his business grew to include over 150 people training out of his office, and he was invited by other offices to train their offices. He was also invited to give motivational speeches at regional conferences. He was not an eloquent speaker! He couldn't pronounce "statistics" if his life depended on it, but his message was uplifting and positive, and his audience believed that even if this great guy didn't know them individually, he believed in them too. He approached his business and his associates with grace and a great positive attitude.

His ideal life is living in the country and playing with his tractor. He still doesn't wear a suit if at all possible. If you meet him on the street, you'd think he was auditioning for ZZ Top. If you see him in a hardware store, you'd think he is an employee. No one would ever guess he is a millionaire. But his success was built on the positive energy he brought to his life and his business and the people he built up and trained. Bring good energy and grace to every aspect of your life and see the amazing results for yourself. Remember it takes practice!!!!

Discussion Questions
1. How would you categorize your energy level?
2. Do you bring positive or negative energy to a group or a situation? What kind changes would you need to make to improve this?
3. How do you initially connect with the people you work with to find out their energy levels and attitudes?
4. How do you assess what needs to be done to bring up the energy level in your group?
5. What do you do in your down time to recharge YOUR energy level?

2

The Art of the Apology

By: Nick Wolff

And you know, when you've experienced grace and you feel like you've been forgiven, you're a lot more forgiving of other people. You're a lot more gracious to others.

~ Rick Warren

Grace in an Apology

When Adam and Eve were sent out from the Garden of Eden, it became known as Original Sin—their fall from Grace. Life after the fall has always been about making amends. When you make a mistake and hurt someone close to you, like Adam and Eve, you strive to make amends. The pursuit of Grace through the power of an apology has echoed through time ever since Eve bit into the apple.

Fathers, Sons, and Unfinished Business

I recently introduced my son to the movie *Field of Dreams*. When I first saw the movie at the age of 12, I thought of it as a baseball movie. The movie features baseball heroes, the novelty of a ballpark in the middle of the cornfield and the amusing situations that emerge when some people see ghosts and others do not. I was, after all, 12 years old. You don't start to see the nuance and subtle messages of the movie until you're much older and have the benefit of life experience.

Fundamentally, *Field of Dreams* is about a son's relationship with his father - a relationship that suffers from a lack of closure. Ray Kinsella, Kevin Costner's character, rebelled against his father. His father was a not quite good enough baseball player that was unable to make his dream of being a professional possible. Like too many fathers, he pressured his son, Ray, to succeed where he couldn't. Ray left home at age 17, hurling insults at his father's hero, Shoeless Joe Jackson, the disgraced White Sox ballplayer, as he left.

It's not unusual for fathers and sons to disagree strongly, sometimes for years. Often though, time and wisdom allow those fathers and sons to transcend those disagreements and validate their love for each other. But someone has to make the first step. Unfortunately for Ray, his father died before either of them decided to take that first step. The last time he saw his father alive, he told his father something terrible and he never allowed himself the opportunity to take it back. He doesn't even realize his remorse until it it's too late to do anything about it. *Field of Dreams* is about a man saying he's sorry to his father through his actions rather than through his words.

Field of Dreams illustrates an important aspect of apologies. The longer an apology goes unsaid, the more profound the apology must be to make it meaningful. Many of our relationships are sullied by unfinished business. Slights, unintended insults, innocuous comments, and miscommunications limit our ability to truly connect with the people in our lives.

Often, we are unwilling to make the first step or don't know how to make it. Little we have to say can help with the first problem. But, if you're willing to make the apology, the tools and techniques in this chapter will assist you. You'll learn to say the right thing and follow through so you, unlike Ray, don't leave unfinished business with the people you love.

SPOTLIGHT ON THE ART OF GRACE

The Great Apologizer

I give great apologies! Even my wife will tell you that. My apologies are well crafted and well delivered. And there's a very good reason why I'm so good at saying I'm sorry. I have had lots of practice.

Recently, I saw an Internet meme about wisdom and how some people of advanced age and have yet to acquire it. My response is that wisdom is not a byproduct of age. Wisdom is the byproduct of having made mistakes and learning from them. Embrace human frailty. The mistakes we make in life, assuming they don't kill us, are invitations to learn - to grow. In my time on this earth, I feel that I have gained some wisdom, but that wisdom was bought with the currency of pain. Part of my penance for my mistakes is to share my lessons with others, in the sincere hope that others will be gracefully spared the unpleasant price I paid.

There is something amazing about watching highly trained athletes, such as ice skaters or gymnasts, as they compete. Their strength, finesse, and body control exude elegance and grace. When I was growing up, I was wholly uncoordinated. I frequently tripped over things. When I tripped, I naturally tried to recover quickly and pretend that the stumble never occurred. But people always notice the stumble and pretending it never happened only made me look more foolish. I have never been physically gifted. I'm not physically graceful, but I have long been driven to become graceful using the equally impressive tools of language, timing, and empathy. Through painstaking effort, I can say that my stumbles in social graces and healing relationships have become less frequent over time. It's with great humility that I hope that my years of work and learning, qualifies me to speak authoritatively about that most important skill - repairing relationships.

A Basketball Hoop on a Sandy Hill

Many people underestimate the power of an apology. There are few things that can more quickly turn around a poor relationship than a sincere and well-crafted apology. Many of the bitterest conflicts can rapidly evolve into much more productive and healthy relationships when someone says they are sorry.

In the mid-1990s, I worked several summers as a member of Boy Scout camp staff. My fellow staffers and I were mostly from the greater Chicago-land area. The staff members were highly diverse from a wide variety of socioeconomic, ethnic, and racial backgrounds. And like a diverse subgroup, there is a tendency for subgroups to form along these traditional boundaries.

SPOTLIGHT ON THE ART OF GRACE

The staff members lived along, "staff row", a long narrow sand dune overlooking the lake that abutted the camp. The staff cabins were situated along one side of the road that led up the centerline of the dune.

Like all property, your cabin could be seen as evidence of hierarchy. At the bottom of the hill were the lowliest of the low, the counselors in training or CITs. These 14 and 15-year-olds were eager but wet behind the ears. They, shall we say, had room to grow. At the top of the hill, we would find the senior staff. These people usually had several years experience as staff members. They had higher profile positions, and were recognized as the camp's leaders among the youth members and staff. In between, the staff members were of varied experience, expertise, and dedication. The further up the slope you were, the closer you were to being part of the 'in crowd'. The further down the hill you were, the closer you were to the dregs of society-- the CITs.

About one third of the way up the hill, were the cabins that were occupied by the black staff members. Note each subgroup on staff row found ways to amuse itself differently. Some of us sat around the fire pit and told stories. Some listened to music, whittled on sticks, or tossed the Frisbee. Some, like the CITs, just sat around and looked pitiful. The black members of staff chose to put up a rudimentary basketball hoop and play one-on-one.

It was actually kind of ingenious. Fashioned out of a long 4 x 4 board, plywood planking, and a milk crate with the bottom cut out, they had a very serviceable homemade basketball hoop. Incidentally, these folks were very good at playing basketball. You have to be. I challenge any reader to try to dribble a ball on a sand dune and tell me how good you will be. But it is that basketball hoop on the sand dune, which is the subject of the story.

As my wife can attest, sometimes men do stupid things - young men all the more so. One evening, for whatever reason, some of our nonblack colleagues from the middle of staff row chose to tear down and throw the basketball hoop into our campfire. Overnight, a stupid action on the part of two of our brothers threatened to erupt into an all-out race war.

Racial tensions in today's America are unproductive and persistent despite huge advances in not only opinions but in actual situations. That being said, the fact that perpetrators of racial crimes, most of whom are long dead, have never and will not ever apologize is a big reason why we still face racial anxiety today.

SPOTLIGHT ON THE ART OF GRACE

Unfortunately, there is not a whole lot we can do about rectifying the sins of the past. But that day - on that sandy hill in 1996 - we chose a different path. We, as a staff, made peace. We apologized for the stupid actions for one of our own. More than that, we built a new basketball hoop even better than the one they had built previously. Afterwards we played the first of several "row-wide" half-court games, of which I can proudly say, I won none. After all, I have a hard enough time dribbling on concrete, much less on sand.

That day was the day we became a staff. Today, the 1996 staff is still considered one of the best in the 100+ year history of the camp.

Why Apologize
Who is the Apology for?
An apology isn't solely for you. Nor is an apology solely for the benefit of others. If you apologize solely for someone else's benefit, it's likely that you won't sound sincere. Your body language and verbal tone will be incongruent with your words. You'll come off patronizing or manipulative. If you apologize solely for your own benefit, it's obvious. You will transmit the reason you're making the apology. If you're afraid of losing the other person, you will seem desperate or jealous. If you're afraid of what others will think of you, you'll

come off as someone with dramatically screwed up priorities. No doubt there are elements of many of these concerns as well as others when you make an apology. But there must be a balance of self-centric and other-centric considerations (biased a bit more toward the other-centric side of the spectrum in my opinion). When it comes to apologies, it is important to remember that an apology is best given for the benefit of you both.

Merriam-Webster defines graciousness as being "marked by kindness and courtesy" as well as "marked by tact and delicacy". In this light, apologies are seen as weapons of mass affection, inflicting graciousness on those colleagues, friends, and lovers that we have trespassed against.

When to Give an Apology

Some people suggest waiting for people to cool off before making an apology. People who want to wait often are trying to rationalize their own escapism - trying to find any way out of doing the unpleasant thing of admitting they screwed up. I would suggest that waiting to make an apology might be the worst strategy you can employ. Raw feelings are a byproduct of a betrayal of the relationship. As an open wound can be cauterized to stop bleeding, the heart works to heal itself by cutting itself off from the source of hurt. The heart works to sever its connection with the threat until no connection is left. As difficult as it is, if you care about healing the relationship, you must act while there's still something left to heal.

My parents were together for 29 years before they ultimately decided to go their separate ways. I have a hard time understanding how you can invest so much of your life in a relationship with a person only to give up on it. But emotional distance can grow even when you sit side by side with another. The powerful force generated by years of slights, sparring, and passive aggressive behavior acts as a wedge prying us from the people we hold dear. It builds a mound of unresolved pain that grows like a mountain. It's rarely one thing that ends a relationship. But it is the last thing that finally starts the avalanche that destroys everything and makes healing impossible.

When you make a mistake, take action as quickly as you can! Every moment you delay their heart is ripping itself away from you. Relationships with friends, parents, children, siblings, and spouses die every day because of the slow death of emotional connections brought about by the sustained decay brought about by unhealed wounds.

Types of Apologies

Apologies come in two flavors. There are relationship maintenance apologies and there are relationship saving apologies. Before discussing these, however, it's important to quickly discuss non-apologies.

The Politician's Apology

Is there anything less sincere than the Politician's Apology?

"I'm sorry to anyone who was offended..."

This is not an apology. This is a statement that someone didn't like what I said and normally I wouldn't care, but because I care about what people think about me, I want to make a show of magnanimity. Worse than recognizing a mistake, accepting ownership of it, and trying to make amends, using the Politician's Apology turns the aggrieved into the aggressor. It essentially says, "It's not my fault that you took offense from something I said or did. You're the overly sensitive, unreasonable rube; and I'm not the least bit sorry."

Remember that an apology must be for the benefit of both people. By its very nature, the Politician's Apology fails.

That is not to say that there aren't serious problems with victim culture. We should be more ready to give people the benefit of the doubt. People usually stumble because of human imperfection rather than malice. But that perspective should inform self-governance rather than our perceptions of others.

In the end, apologies are hard work. Good apologies are exercises in grace and craftsmanship. If we are going to make an apology, we should do it right. Invest the time, the sincerity and, the personal vulnerability to maximize the chance the apology will hit the mark. If you are unwilling to invest the effort, it may be better to avoid apologizing. Poorly crafted apologies are likely to do more harm than good.

<u>Relationship Maintaining Apologies</u>
Last week I was driving with my wife to the store. When I rolled into the parking stall, I didn't provide much room for her to open the door. I knew I had just made my wife's life just a little bit harder. I said, "I'm sorry. I didn't mean to do that." She smiled and said, "That's okay."

Many of us frequently tell those we care about, "I love you". Saying 'I love you' is a ritual. It provides consistent validation that someone holds a special place in your heart. We do it so routinely that we often hardly realize we're doing it. It's

THE ART OF THE APOLOGY

something just done to maintain the relationship. Similarly, we often find ourselves apologizing in a similar way. When we do something that's ill considered or ungenerous, when we realize the mistake, we will immediately apologize. It demonstrates graciousness and the fact that no insult or slight was intended. These relationship maintenance apologies serve to provide validation to others that we care about them and want to ensure that our loved ones have no reason to believe otherwise.

These Relationship Maintaining apologies serve two vital roles. First, as was said, relationship maintaining apologies provide reassurance to people that the relationship is strong. Secondly, and perhaps more importantly, these quick apologies, wash away the little hurts we can inadvertently inflict upon those we care about. These apologies clear away the baggage that collects between you so that the pile does not become a mountain. It is the psychological distance created by a mountain of baggage between two people serving as the wedge driving them apart. The best way to hold on to the people you love is to not allow the wedge to exist in the first place.

Relationship maintaining apologies work best when they are done immediately after you realize the mistake. Despite being a ploy to maintain a relationship, these apologies still must be delivered with sincerity. It's still important to be truly sorry for the mistake. Another definition of grace is "to confer dignity or honor," but there is no dignity in insincerity.

Amanda's story

Unbeknownst to me I had really pissed Amanda off. Amanda had been a fairly close friend of mine. In my first year at the University of Illinois, she and I had both been in the same dorm complex. We had both decided to join the same organization which is how I got to know her and become friends with her. About a year later, Amanda and I were at a party. At this party, I got tipsy and said something awfully stupid and hurtful. Twenty-two-year-olds tend to do that sort of thing.

At the party was a particularly obnoxious fellow. He was a five-foot-four ball of muscle that joined the wrestling team to compensate for his Napoleon complex. He seemed to me to be arrogant and hotheaded. During the course of the evening, however, Amanda had gotten close to him. It was apparent that they were interested in each other. As the party went on, I had more beers and I had the opportunity to interact with the wrestler a bit more. My opinion of him diminished still more. I honestly didn't understand what she saw in the guy. But it wasn't my place to insinuate myself into her decisions or to judge her for them. That was my mistake. When the wrestler went off to the restroom, I leaned over to Amanda and asked her, "What's with that guy? He is such a jerk!" Amanda went on to defend him, "I think he seems like really nice guy." And then I said it. "I just lost all respect for you." As I recall it now, I see the words reach out of my mouth in the shape of a giant foam hand, wind up, and smack Amanda right across the face.

Over the years, I have found that I can say very dumb and insensitive things while drinking. It's the primary reason why I do it so rarely - drinking that is - not saying dumb and insensitive things.

Several months went by. During this time, I had become extremely busy with schoolwork and had not been seeing much of anybody. Amanda and I rarely saw each other. This made sense, I thought. We were, after all, in different colleges on completely different sides of the campus. Nevertheless, I missed my friend. Whenever I did see her, although always cordial, I began to notice that there was a chill in the relationship that hadn't been there before. Over time I chalked it up to the all too common ebbing of friendship that comes with distance and lack of nurturing. Sorry to say that that happens more often in my life than I would like.

Little did I know how much damage that I had inadvertently caused to our relationship. It certainly wasn't my intention to cause her harm. But that's the thing about matters of the heart. When it comes to the relationships with the people we care about, you don't get points for your intentions. My intended throwaway comment turned out to be much more hurtful than I had ever realized. I had unwittingly ended a relationship with a good friend.

As luck would have it, the demon liquor became the angel in the end. Just two months prior to her graduation, and my subsequent enrollment in graduate school, Amanda and I were again at a party together. Armed with the additional year of experience, I must say that my behavior hadn't evolved much. Again, Amanda and I had gotten tipsy and were again in a quiet room chatting a bit like we had used to do. It is true that alcohol makes you speak more freely and honestly. I spoke too freely that night the previous year and was about to discover that I had done so. During the conversation, after about a half an hour of catching up and laughing, the conversation took a dramatic turn. She expressed to me just how much I hurt her. I was floored. It never had occurred to me that the chill of the relationship that I had perceived was something that I caused. I also made a quick realization that if she was bringing about a year later, it must have been a wound that she still carried with her. Needless to say, the rest of the party for me didn't go very well. As I sat quietly in a deserted corner of the house where the party was going on, internally I was stewing in a dark elixir equal parts shock and remorse.

There's a great deal of wisdom in giving apology as soon as possible. I'll discuss that later. But in this case, the wound had been open for a year. Giving apologies is an urgent matter. But there's a difference between urgent and hasty. I needed time to sit down and craft this carefully if I was going to succeed in salvaging my friendship with Amanda. I recall spending no less than four hours the next day crafting my note to her. The contents of the email are for Amanda and I alone. I will only say that I took complete ownership of my mistake. I told her that I cared for her and wanted a relationship with her. Finally, I told her that I had surrendered the right to expect to retain her friendship, but that I hoped she would choose to remain my friend.

Amanda carried the wound I obliviously left her with for over a year. I had no right to expect her to respond to my apology. It's a testament to her generous spirit and her enormous heart that she chose to reconnect with me. And I will be forever grateful to her for the grace she extended to me. We still chat from time to time. I value her friendship. She is rather accomplished as an author these days and we support each other in our writing. It would've been a shame to lose the benefit of her wisdom over the years. However, it would have been more of a tragedy if she were to have continued to carry that injury a single day more.

Relationship Saving Apologies

I had to prepare and deliver a relationship saving apology to win back Amanda's friendship. These are the apologies that you deliver after a major screw-up. Many of us have done stupid or insensitive things that have obviously hurt others or have seriously threatened someone's trust in us. In these situations, apologies must be crafted in a careful and considered manner. Relationship Saving apologies are intended to repair the relationship. To be effective, they must give full treatment to all the aspects of an apology. They must fully acknowledge the mistake that was made and take appropriate ownership of the mistake. Relationship Saving apologies must reestablish the bonds of caring and concern and establish safeguards to ensure that similar violations will not happen in the future. Finally, these types of apologies must humbly ask for forgiveness.

Remember that though it's important to hope for forgiveness, one should never expect to be forgiven. Ultimately the choice of forgiveness lies with the one that was hurt.

Few relationships can survive several critical hits no matter how well crafted the apology. It's simply unhealthy for people to associate with those who hurt them repeatedly. There are countless stories of serial abusers who have fits of rage only to become genuinely sorry after the damage has been done. Mistakes must be corrected. If changing behavior is beyond one's ability, one who truly cares about others who have been hurt should conclude that what is best for others is for them to be separated from the source of pain. The plain truth is that if I can't provide for your safety going forward, any apology I make is going to be insincere at its heart. Since Relationship Saving apologies are only performed after a major break in trust, they really can only be performed once.

Relationship Saving apologies must be elaborate, heartfelt, and vulnerable. They are some of the most difficult conversations one can have. But, if crafted and delivered with sincerity, heart, and grace, they can lead to even closer relationships going forward.

Crafting Apologies

Functional Components of Effective Apologies

There are five main functional components of effective apologies. They are:

- Acknowledgment
- Taking ownership
- Validating the relationship
- Establishing assurances
- The ask

Each of these components is discussed in greater detail in the succeeding paragraphs.

Acknowledgment

The first thing apology has to do is to acknowledge the error. To be effective, an apology must be perceived as sincere. No apology will be seen as sincere if the error is not identified or if the speaker really doesn't think it's an error. This is where the Politician's Apology is so counterproductive. The Politician's Apology implies that the speaker doesn't really believe that a mistake occurred. Before you start to craft an apology, clarify! Clarify! Clarify! Ask questions to be sure you understand your mistake. Sometimes hurts extend to multiple levels. Be sure to probe others to ensure you have a full understanding of the mistake.

There is more to acknowledgment than simply identifying the error, however. I moved to Omaha, Nebraska in 2010. I accepted a job leading a division at a local engineering consultancy. Unbeknownst to me, this firm had developed quite a poor reputation in the local market over the years. Service errors, quality problems, disagreements, and poor communication practices had sullied the firm's reputation. For the first year I was there, my job was essentially to be a professional apologizer. I drove around town trying to mend the fences that others had ripped down. The thing about hurt feelings is that they are emotional in their very nature. Intellectually, the men and women sitting across from me at a table knew that I was not responsible for the mistakes of previous leaders, but that did little to soothe their emotional scars. But without soothing those scars, renewal of the relationship would be impossible. How do you craft apologies to sincerely atone for the actions of others? This challenge led me to one of the most important insights into acknowledgment - empathy. Acknowledgment is not just about admitting the mistake that was made. It's also about acknowledging the emotional journey that the other person made in response to that mistake. I was able to crawl into the shoes of the other person and acknowledge the hurt, frustration, annoyance, and betrayal that they felt. This shared emotional experience forges emotional bonds between people. It allows people to get past those emotions and become open to new possibilities.

Take Ownership

Closely associated with identifying the mistake, the next step in an apology is to take ownership of the mistake. Avoid language such as, "mistakes were made". In our culture, we've been taught the importance of helping others save face. This face-saving notion is even more powerful in non-Western cultures. It is not considered a social nicety to assign blame. But, we often overlook the personal power that comes from accepting blame. Because so few people in the society actually accept blame, partly in response to increased litigation, people are caught off guard and often impressed when people actually do. When you make a mistake, use assertive language to admit ownership of the mistake. It's much more meaningful for people to hear, "I messed up," rather than, "I'm sorry that happened to you".

One of the biggest challenges that coming from taking ownership of mistakes is what to do when the mistakes really aren't yours or, perhaps, there were no mistakes at all. It's worthwhile to examine these two topics.

As I was driving around town apologizing for the actions of my predecessors, I mentioned that I was struggling with how to atone for the actions of others. While emotional acknowledgment is extremely helpful, people do want to hear the words, "I'm sorry". But if the mistake truly is yours, how do you genuinely say you're sorry? In this case, be the company man. Chances are if you are in a position where you must apologize, you likely enjoy some organizational leadership or responsibility. You always have the agency of your role to act on behalf of the larger organization. Apologize on its behalf.

Of course, sometimes people observe things that really aren't mistakes, but others perceive them as such. If you feel you are justified and don't believe a mistake was made, how do you sincerely craft an apology? Often times, all that is necessary to sooth the raw emotions of others, is to take a little bit of responsibility. In these cases, you should take the appropriate level of responsibility, but no more. Appropriate means that you admit fault to the extent that you made a mistake - and there was one. Even in those cases where you feel like you performed flawlessly and the actions that were taken were perfectly justifiable, obviously certain expectations were set or perceptions were not dispelled that allowed someone to arrive at the conclusion that they did. If nothing else, you can find fault in yourself here. Apologize for the mistake that you made. Do not accept responsibility for more than what was appropriate. This way you can be assertive in your own perspective while remaining considerate of others.

Validate Relationship

Acknowledging mistakes and, taking ownership of them, acts like a huge bulldozer pushing all the accumulated crap out of the way. Having cleared the air and washed away the baggage, it is time to lay the groundwork for rebuilding the relationship. Take time to acknowledge how important the individual and the relationship with him or her is to you. Then, outline your hopes for the relationship going forward. Make the case that should the other person decide to accept the apology, good things are around the corner.

Establish assurances

Obviously the biggest concern one might have would be to protect oneself going forward. Therefore, when apologizing, don't just say that whatever bad thing happened in the past will be repeated, give concrete reasons as to why. What safeguards are being put in place to offer protection and prevention? How will you monitor yourself to ensure you don't fall back into bad habits? What are some tangible milestones that will help the other person track your progress? The assurances and the mechanisms that support them provide the foundation for rebuilding trust.

The Ask

Ultimately, in order to be forgiven, you'll need to ask for forgiveness. Your job is to humbly express a desire to maintain a relationship. If they share that desire, they'll respond. If they don't, you can at least part knowing you've done everything you could to make amends. You can leave with a clear conscience.

The Four R's

Despite popular wisdom, sticks and stones have nothing on words. Words hurt! When it comes to crafting apologies or with regard to anything associated with interpersonal conflict, there is a useful construct that has served me well over the years. All interpersonal conflict is played out over four dimensions. These four dimensions are summarized as the 4R's:

- Respect,
- Relationship,
- Reputation, and
- Restitution.

SPOTLIGHT ON THE ART OF GRACE

The first three elements concern the presence in the future. Restitution is bound the past - making up for a screw up. When people are getting along, the first three are humming along and there's no need for the fourth. This means respect, relationship, and reputation become the three Commandments of good relationship maintenance.

My hurtful comments to Amanda broke all three at once. I insinuated myself amid her relationships. I told her I had no respect for her. And I said this publicly in front of all of our friends at a party. It was as if I had taken a flamethrower to our relationship.

On rare occasions, it may be forgivable to insinuate yourself into the relationship to somebody else, particularly if you're concerned about one's safety and wellbeing. Since this tactic is not without its risks, it should be avoided whenever possible. The disrespect, coupled with public repudiation, was inexcusable under any circumstances. The comment was a relationship killer. My seemingly throwaway comment was actually a scythe ripping right to her heart.

The Hardest Apology

I began this chapter discussing the movie *Field of Dreams* – the story of Ray Kinsella, whose father passed away before

Ray had the chance to apologize. The hardest apologies are those apologies that we will never have the chance to deliver.

When my son was six years old, I received a phone call from our daycare provider. I was told there was a problem in that I had to come immediately to pick him up. When I arrived, I learned that he had gotten upset, thrown a tantrum, had broken a glass cabinet door. I was very upset. But then they brought me to see my son, and I wasn't upset anymore. He was shaking and weeping uncontrollably. I sat down on the floor across from him and asked him to look up and meet my eyes. His expression betrayed the combination of fear and mortification. He said over and over, "I didn't mean to do that." I saw that expression and my heart melted. I had seen those eyes before - in a mirror.

When I was 14 years old, I was at a large Fourth of July barbecue at the house of one of my father's friends. As the oldest kid the grown-ups gave me charge over some fireworks. My parents were chitchatting with their friends while several of the other children and I let off fireworks in the middle of the park. Several weeks prior I was visiting family in another state. We had taken to having fireworks fights, launching bottle rockets at each other. We even thought it was fun, when we broke off the little wooden sticks to help guide the bottle rockets. It added uncertainty. We had no idea where they would go. And it was fun. I was using the same technique for bottle rockets at this barbecue. It was fun. But I grabbed a larger skyrocket. I figured that since it was so much fun doing this with a bottle rocket, it will be even more fun doing it with the skyrocket. So I broke off the large wooden shaft and lit the fuse. The skyrocket lifted into the air. Like the bottle rocket, the skyrocket's path was uncertain. It eventually turned and aimed itself at a young lady who had been sitting with her family on a lawn chair at the edge of the park. It wasn't fun anymore.

Fifteen minutes later when the ambulance hauled her away, I was overcome with the same set of emotions that I knew my son was now dealing with. I never knew what happened to the poor lady. Did she lose an eye? Did she make a full recovery? Sometimes, I consider the possibility that I actually killed her. The sad part is that I will never know. I have to live with that. Since that day long ago, I have never been able to enjoy the Fourth of July, more specifically fireworks. Yet I am a father. Kids like fireworks on the Fourth of July. I do my duty as a father, though I take no pleasure in it. That is my penance. I know the burden of Ray Kinsella feels. The hardest apology is the one that you cannot deliver.

In the years since, I've made attempts to atone for my mistake. I have never engaged in the reckless behaviors of many of my cohorts. I'm too familiar with the terrible price that can be paid.

All of these thoughts and images flashed in my head as I sat eye-to-eye with my son. He sat there crying, perhaps dreading what I was going to say or do. All I did was grab him, and hug him tightly. I picked him up, walked him out the door, and set him down next to me on the curb. I took the time to reassure him that I was not mad. I told him I knew he felt bad. I told him to use this as a lesson. I told him to remember the price that mistakes can carry and that it's important to think and to avoid being swept up in the moment. That's when mistakes happen.

It's true that as we get older, our power to hurt others and ourselves through our mistakes increases. As we drove back home, I actually was thankful that my boy had the opportunity to learn this lesson at such a young age, when his power to hurt was limited to a $200 glass door. We all should be so lucky. I hope he carries this lesson going forward. Maybe he will be spared the lifetime guilt that his father carries.

Conclusion

Apologies are essential tools in maintaining and saving relationships with members of a group. Crafting and delivering apologies well are a foundational skill set in wielding grace in a group. It is my hope that the techniques discussed in this chapter will serve you well as continue to grow and enhance relationships with you colleagues, cohorts, and loved ones.

Discussion Questions

1. Recall a time when you delivered an apology well. How did you incorporate the lessons in this chapter?
2. Draft an apology using the 5-part framework discussed in this chapter.
3. Consider a time when an apology didn't have the intended effect? How would have the experience gone differently by using the techniques outlined in this chapter?
4. Think about a recent conflict situation you observed. How is the 4R framework represented?
5. What wisdom have you gained through your mistakes? How has that wisdom informed your life?
6. In what ways does the multifaceted notion of grace intersect with an apology?
7. What unfinished business do you have? Create action plans to finish it.

3

Take No Offense

By: Gloria Harmon

"Those who were able to forgive their former enemies were able also to return to the outside world and rebuild their lives, no matter what the physical scars. Those who nursed their bitterness remained invalids. It was as simple and as horrible as that."

~ Corrie ten Boom

How do you perceive offense? Do you feel that you have to defend yourself? Can you show class in a situation of offense?

Let's start with a definition: Offense means to be hurt, angry or upset at something or someone. Offense is that feeling of rage over a perceived injustice. The mind continually replays the offense increasing in its intensity as you dwell on it. The art of grace in this situation is to bring every thought captive to "whatsoever things are honest, just, pure, lovely, of good report, if there be any virtue or praise, then think on these things." "Philippians 4: 8 KJV." Think of it like this, I must change what I am thinking in order to stop the hurt, and anger that is going on in my mind.

Those negative feelings, if allowed to fester, start becoming a belief system which will, in time, become what I start speaking. What I start speaking in time will lead to negative feelings. My negative feelings may lead to negative actions. Our minds are very powerful. It has been proven that what you think affects your body. People in athletics usually visualize themselves winning before they physically win an event. Instead of taking offense, why not think in the positive and see yourself accomplishing the goals that you have set or completing that dream? The same energy needed to think in the negative you can now use to think in the positive and actually accomplish far more.

Offense is driven by fear. I can choose not to fear. I can choose to change situations around me by what I choose to think and do.

Many times people with anger issues have greater amounts of illnesses than those who are more positive. Negative thoughts on a continuous basis bring about depression, insecurity, fear, anger, frustration, and, in some cases, mental illness just to name a few outcomes that are not so good.

Many times those who are offended become oppressive. They will use force or intimidation to get people to do what they say. Oppression devalues life. The goal is to make everyone feel just as insecure and fearful as the oppressor. People who oppress need someone who they perceive is in a worse condition than they are.

Instead of being sucked in by the insecurity and fear of others, I choose to walk in love. I choose to treat others the way I want to be treated. It is inspiring to me to have people follow me because I inspire them as opposed to people following me because of intimidation and fear.

Who really is the greatest leader? It will always be the leader who inspires others. Usually, when an offense is taken, the concern is how others will perceive you. How about rewriting the standard on perception and changing the standard to doing what is right? I think it would be phenomenal to make every decision based on "is this right" then do it or "is this wrong" then don't do it.

Brother Francis's Story

It is at this point that I would like to introduce you to Brother Francis who is from Tanzania, Africa. He is associated with the ministry of Heidi Baker. Meetings were being held at a compound in Tanzania and Brother Francis was monitoring the gate. The meeting was about to begin so Francis started shutting the gate. About that time, four men walked up to him and he thought they were coming to the meeting. The four men grabbed him and said we are going to beat you to death. At this point, they started beating him. The men ran away and left Brother Francis in a puddle of blood and badly swollen from the beating.

A ministry member found him and called an ambulance. He was taken to a hospital. Everyone at the meeting on the compound immediately started praying for Brother Francis. Meanwhile, at the hospital, he was pronounced dead from the beating. Then something miraculous happened. Brother Francis came back to consciousness. The people at the compound continued to pray for Brother Francis and the next morning another miracle happened, all the swelling was gone from his face and body. The hospital released Brother

TAKE NO OFFENSE

Francis, the man that they had pronounced dead the night before. Everyone at the compound was praying also for the police to catch and prosecute the men who did such a horrible thing. The police did catch one of the guys and put him in jail.

When Brother Francis returned to the compound the next day, there was great rejoicing for the miracle of life for Brother Francis. Everyone also, rejoiced that one of the guys who committed this crime was captured. Brother Francis left the compound and went to the police station. He asked that the guy who committed the crime be released because he was not pressing charges against him. Everyone at the police station was stunned. At first, no one believed him, but Brother Francis convinced the police and they released the guy. When Brother Francis saw the guy he said: "I forgive you and I love you." Francis gave the man a big hug. The man was so moved at how Brother Francis handled the situation that he gave his life to Christ and is now preaching the gospel.

My question is: could Francis have been offended? Many would even say he had a right to be offended with the guys who had beaten him to death. Who really is the victor? Who not only changed the situation but also changed countless lives because he refused to be offended. Who really had the greater power? Who showed true leadership? Brother Francis showed the art of grace.

When we seek to get revenge, there comes with that decision fear, insecurity, loss of peace and in many cases loss of health as a result of negative thoughts and actions. The human body was not designed to carry negative thoughts and actions continually. It is foreign to our original purpose, which is to love God, Love one another, and love your self. When we make the decision to take no offense, we have peace because we trust God to do judgment and justice on our behalf to those who wronged us. The one thing that is amazing about God is that he never judges or does justice out of hate or anger. He always judges from the standpoint of His unending love. His goal is always to turn hearts and minds back to Him, back to righteousness. The stringent judgment is only after every attempt has been made to turn mankind back to righteousness.

Corrie ten Boom's Story

Let's look at another powerful example of where taking no offense resulted in many hearts changing for the better, not to mention, the freedom that comes from forgiveness. The individual forgiving is released from the weight of carrying an offense and thinking of ways to get back at people. Sometimes the people involved do not even remember the offense, but we choose to hang on to things for generations and people do not even remember what happened because it has been so long.

Now for the story of Corrie ten Boom. Corrie was fifty years old when the Nazis invaded Holland. Her family members were devout Christians. Her father owned a watch shop. When the family, Corrie, her sister and her father, saw what was happening to the Jews, they knew that they had to do something. The family had a secret room built that they used for hiding the Jews to preserve their lives. The Jews would stay for a short time and then be moved to a series of safe houses until the Dutch underground could smuggle them out of the country. Their belief was so strong that they chose to risk their lives to save the lives of God's chosen people.

Eventually, the family was turned in to the German Gestapo and the family was taken to a concentration camp. The Gestapo never found the Jews that were in the house at the time. They were safely taken to another safe house. Corrie's family, however, did not fare so well. Corrie's father died in prison and her sister died in a concentration camp. Corrie survived the prison, a work camp, and was in a concentration camp scheduled for execution. She was released from the concentration camp because of a clerical error made in the spelling of her name.

After release from the concentration camp, and after the war ended, Corrie had a new direction for her life and that was traveling all over the world talking to people about the healing and freedom that comes from taking no offense and forgiving. At one meeting, Corrie was strongly tested in what she was sharing about taking no offense and forgiveness. A man, who had been a guard at the concentration camp, where she and her sister were assigned, came forward. Corrie remembered his cruelty, and the beatings that were given her sister at his hands. He did not recognize Corrie, but she did recognize him. He came forward and asked for forgiveness for all his cruel actions towards Jews during the war.

At that moment, she had to decide what she was going to do. Was she going to walk in love? Or would her emotions rule her and keep her bound to her past? Would she be a victim or a victor? What decision would you make in this situation? Would you take the hand that was extended? This was the guard that had been cruel to Corrie and her sister. This was the man she helplessly watched as he beat her beloved sister. The world would say Corrie had every right to be angry and to stay angry. "An eye for an eye" was the first thought that came to

Corrie. However, Corrie chose to do what she had encouraged others to do to truly be free. She extended her hand to the former guard, and allowing them both to receive healing, forgiveness, and freedom from the past. As a result of her courageous step, doors of opportunity started opening wider for Corrie. She wrote a book detailing her experiences during the war called *The Hiding Place*. It sold millions of copies. She also had a movie made based on her book, *The Hiding Place*. Who showed the art of grace? Who showed real class?

Every day of our lives we make decisions. Some decisions are minor and some are major but eventually, any decision has a negative or positive consequence. How much can we change the world around us by making the decision to always choose the higher road, the road where we choose to take no offense? How many lives have already been lost to individuals or groups taking offense and dwelling on the offense until it becomes a mindset? That mindset is then vocalized. Usually, from becoming vocal, actions follow. What would happen in a short amount of time if opposing forces choose to take no offense and choose to find common ground? What if we did not feel that we must be in control? How about our promoting self-control?

SPOTLIGHT ON THE ART OF GRACE

There are vital things that every group of people throughout all mankind find important. What would happen in a short amount of time if our youth saw adults taking no offense and willing to forgive to receive peace, healing, and freedom from the past? What is even more surprising is that many times after centuries and generations of teaching offense no one really remembers what the original offense entailed. I am amazed at how easy it is to get offended people together in a group to complain and not offer any positive solutions, but always finding ways to band together for evil.

What would happen if we choose to be grace in a group? What would happen if we choose to be true leaders and agents of change? What would happen if people's perception of us were not a factor in our choosing to take no offense or even reacting in a negative way? Would the majority of us choose to act differently if we were not trying to fit into what we think someone else wants us to be or do? What would happen to our thinking, our words, and our actions if we decided to be grace in a group starting today? Our world would suddenly become a different place.

<u>Tamar's Story</u>

Another example of where offense and not forgiving were being held onto like it was a God-given right is the story of

Absalom, the very handsome son of King David of Israel. Absalom had an equally beautiful younger sister called Tamar. Tamar's beauty was unsurpassed.

To better understand why certain events happen, I will give some details on the chain reaction of consequences that come when people, especially a leader, think they are doing something in secret. It happened that King David was on his roof when he saw a most beautiful woman taking a bath on her roof, which was lower than his. Instead of diverting his attention and mind, King David kept looking and started to lust for this woman. Upon asking his servants about this woman, he learned that the woman was the wife of one of his most trusted and loyal leaders in his army.

This was a man who David had helped to train, and he had mentored to become an experienced, well-polished, fighting machine. This is a man that David had placed in leadership, because of his courage and ethics. Uriah was the soldier's name. He had been with David for years as they ran through caves fighting, and running from King Saul. This loyal friend's wife, Bathsheba, was the woman David started to lust after.

SPOTLIGHT ON THE ART OF GRACE

David was a man who had many wives and concubines and, as king, he could call upon any virgin of the kingdom to be his wife or concubine. David had sent his army on a military campaign. As a result, Bathsheba's husband was not around.

David sent his servant to go get Bathsheba and he lay with her. Later, Bathsheba told him that she was pregnant. David's first thought was to cover up what he had done. David's first idea was to bring Bathsheba's husband, Uriah, back from the fighting and have him go home to his wife, whom he had not seen in months. David thought that everyone would then think that the child that Bathsheba conceived was Uriah's. King David called for Uriah to return home and asked him about the fighting and how it had been going. He had a beautiful meal prepared for Uriah and served him plenty of wine until he was very drunk. David then told Uriah to go home to his wife. He thought that his plan was exceptional since Uriah had not seen his beautiful wife in months.

To David's surprise, Uriah was found the next morning on the doorsteps of the palace sleeping. When King David asked Uriah the next morning why he had not gone home to his wife, Uriah answered and said all my mighty fighting men are out on the battlefield fighting and sleeping on the ground.

TAKE NO OFFENSE

How can I come home to comfort while they are at war? "…As thou liveth, and thy soul liveth, I will not do this thing" "2Sam11: 11 KJV".

King David is now in panic mode because someone is bound to find out that he has been with Bathsheba since he could not get Uriah to go home. David's last resort was to have Uriah killed. King David wrote a note to his general and had Uriah deliver the note. In the note, the general was to put Uriah in a position of heavy fighting. He was then to pull the troops back and leave Uriah unprotected so that he would be killed. King David ended the note by saying, "let me know when Uriah is dead."

After getting word of Uriah's death, Bathsheba mourned the required amount of time, then, married King David. Now no one would know of King David's sin. However, God knew of King David's sin and sent the prophet Nathan to confront King David. The prophet told a parable of a rich man who stole a lamb from a poor man. The poor man only had the one lamb.

When King David heard of this grave injustice, he was furious and said that this rich man should be killed for what he did. The prophet told the King that he was the rich man.

SPOTLIGHT ON THE ART OF GRACE

Fortunately, King David confessed his sin and asked forgiveness. God did forgive King David, however, because King David caused the death of Uriah and also married his wife, "Now, therefore, the sword shall never depart from thine house." This judgment was on King David's generations.

Now we go back to Absalom and his beautiful sister Tamar. King David had many wives and many concubines. All of his wives were around him. All of his children were around him. They lived in different houses with their mothers but they all knew that they were related. Beautiful Tamar had a half-brother who started lusting after her (like King David lusted after Bathsheba.) Her half-brother Ammon lusted so much that he made himself sick. One of Ammon's cousins and best friend asked Ammon why he was sick and so sad. He finally confessed that he longed after his beautiful sister Tamar.

It was at this time that Ammon and his cousin devised a plan for Ammon to have Tamar his sister. Their plan was for Ammon to pretend to be sicker than he really was in his body. He then sent a messenger to his father King David asking him if Tamar could come to cook and feed him a meal to help him recover. King David approved the request of his son and Tamar was sent to her brother's house.

TAKE NO OFFENSE

After she fixed the meal and tried to feed her brother Ammon, he would not eat instead he ordered all the servants to leave the house. Ammon then raped his sister Tamar. Tamar fought and pleaded with her brother Ammon but to no avail. After he raped her, he then hated her as much as he had once loved her. He did not even want to be around her. He then took Tamar and her ripped clothes and kicked her out of his house and locked the door.

The beautiful Tamar threw dirt on her head as a sign of disgrace. She left with uncontrollable tears running down her face. She went to her full-blood brother Absalom's house in shame. Her brother Absalom comforted her. Absalom waited to see what his father King David would do upon hearing what had happened. King David did nothing other than telling Ammon that what he did was wrong. Meanwhile, the beautiful Tamar's life was in shambles. Absalom took offense, but said and did nothing for three years.

At the end of three years when everyone thought that everything was back to normal and everyone was on good terms, Absalom gave a great feast for all of his brothers. Everyone was making merry and enjoying each other's company when Absalom grabbed a sword and killed his brother Ammon. Of course, everyone ran, jumped on their donkey and fled, not knowing what was happening or why. The first report that King David received was that all of his sons were dead. The next report that King David received was that his son Ammon was the only one killed.

King David's sons all went to the palace to their father. King David along with his sons cried bitterly. He was told that Absalom had killed Ammon. Also, he learned that Absalom had fled to another country. Absalom had held onto offense and not forgiveness for three years before taking revenge. This offense tore at the very fabric of King David's family in every generation.

<u>Humility</u>

Taking no offense involves huge doses of bible humility. Humility to me is being in perfect obedience to God's will for you at any given time. To be in obedience you must trust that the Living God is the same today, yesterday and forever. I feel that David the shepherd boy was being very humble when he came to the troops of Israel and heard and saw Goliath defile the army of the Living God. He humbled himself at the leading of the spirit of God in him and went up against Goliath. In "2 Chronicles 7:14 KJV", the Living God tells us how to act at any given time to get Him to come to our defense. There are numerous scriptures proving this point.

The verse reads, "If my people, which are called by my name, shall humble themselves, and pray, and seek my face, and turn from their wicked ways; then will I hear from heaven, and I will forgive their sin, and will heal their land."

I had not really focused on humility until asked to do this chapter on taking no offense and forgiveness. I then realized that throughout the scriptures when there was disobedience, and a nation was in great peril, the common thread that turned the tide was the people of the Living God repenting, praying, and seeking the face of the Living God through Christ Jesus. Throughout the scriptures, the words "they humbled themselves before God" are written and God always showed up. We must learn to trust the Living God. That is accomplished through trusting Him enough to do what He says. This is called humility. True humility is placing our trust in the Living God that He will be true to His Word.

Great leaders all through history have called this nation to prayer when things seemed very bleak. Every single time this was done, situations changed in our favor. Great leaders of other countries have done the same and seen situations turn favorable to them. Have we become a nation that intellectually feels that we are too smart to believe in or trust the Creator of all things?

Do we honestly believe that creation happened by chance? Are we too stiff-necked to get on our knees in humility, and confess our sins and repent to the only Living God who has a proven track record of changing situations? Do we honestly believe that we have all the answers? Can we rationalize away Divine Intervention on our behalf that comes from humility, a trust in God? When will we as a nation humble ourselves and seek the face of the Living God? How many times in my personal life have I called upon the name of the Lord and He heard my prayer and answered it? In my young, ignorant days, I would start rationalizing away God's intervention on my behalf because I was concerned about how other people would perceive it. The faithfulness of the Living God became luck or a coincidence.

It was not until I started learning about whom I am that people's opinions of me did not matter as much. This is especially true if those opinions do not line up with the Word of the Living God. I had to start studying seriously to find out what truth really is. I had to start understanding what His Word was saying as well as looking at the patterns and prophecies across hundreds of years that were matching up. This process is very humbling because I had to make every effort to start reading through the Bible every year. What I realized is that I am forever learning and, to me that is exciting. This process has made the Living God more tangible and more personal to me. We are in a time when there are excellent teachers of the Bible and many are very gifted in teaching certain sections or themes within the Bible. This has brought so much more clarity to scriptures.

The greatest key in humility is to actually do what the spirit of God in you tells you to do at any given time; it is not necessarily the same thing that another person is told to do. But, you will have a compelling urge to do something. For different people, the compelling urge may be different or it may be in partnership with someone else for a desired end for the betterment of mankind. For example, it may be like the young man who started collecting backpacks and toiletries for Foster Children to help them as they transition to a new temporary home. In time, this young man had people giving donations from all over the country. For King David, some of his compelling things to do were to design and build musical instruments, to train up and mentor leaders, and to set up kingdom protocol.

Dr. George Washington Carver's Story
I guess one of the best examples of humility in our modern day times would be Dr. George Washington Carver. I see Dr.

SPOTLIGHT ON THE ART OF GRACE

Carver's life as a man who listened to the compelling urges from God to create over three hundred uses for the peanut. Because of the depletion of the nutrients in the soil from constantly growing cotton, and the infestation of the boll weevil in the southern states that destroyed the cotton plants, the economy had almost been totally destroyed. Dr. George Washington Carver's work ethic and humility, before the living God, helped to save the economy of the southern states from certain failure. He was a very humble man and made no secret of his going to God for the answers to the problems facing agriculture in the south. Dr. Carver had a mobile laboratory called the Jessup wagon. This mobile lab was a classroom on wheels. The Jessup wagon gave Dr. Carver the ability to teach and train farmers how to improve their soil and their crops. He encouraged many farmers to start planting peanuts. Dr. Carver was not looking for fortune or fame. His desire was to help the down trodden. His humility showed through. He turned down offers from some of the most well known and wealthiest men in his time to stay true to what he felt the Living God had called him do in his lifetime.

To Conclude

The art of grace is to take no offense, and to walk in forgiveness and humility. This is the highest form of showing class. As I reflect on the lives and legacies of the individuals that I gave as examples I can't help but wonder in amazement at the effect these individuals had on so many other lives in ways that literally changed mindsets and produced positive actions and reactions.

With brother Francis of Tanzania, through his genuine display of love, countless hundreds of lives have found salvation and peace through the ministry of the man who along with others beat him to death. When I look at Corrie Tin-Boon, I see the sheer strength and tenacity it took to look a one-time adversary in the face and call him brother. What she did changed generations in the one-time guard's family and changed a situation from hate to love. This is how you truly make a difference in our world. A look at King David shows how one indiscretion, and a secret sin to cover the indiscretion tore at the fabric of his family. We saw the trickle-down effect of sin on future generations. We see Absalom, King David's son, so filled with offense against his half-brother that it drove him to murder him then flee to another country away from family and friends. He had exiled himself.

Absalom eventually came back to his homeland still filled with offense and hate that led him to try and overthrow his father's rule. This attempt was unsuccessful and resulted in his death. Also, we see in history that Absalom's children did not have a heart for God. That was Absalom's legacy.

We see King David's humanness, but more importantly, we see his love for the Lord God. King David always ran toward the Lord God and repented of his sins. Even God said he was a man after His own heart. I showed how humility is a part of taking no offense and forgiveness. I showed how obeying what the Lord God tells you to do is the highest form of humility. When we are obedient to the call or gifting in our lives, that is the art of grace. Our refusing to let the perceptions of others and our refusing to take offense usually have an affect on our generations in a positive way. This is how to build a legacy for future generations.

When I look at Dr. George Washington Carver, I see a true superhero. He overcame every adversity and challenge in life with class and dignity. He was a man focused on his purpose and gifts in life and accomplished every goal in excellence. His gifts truly did make room for him and took him before kings.

Discussion Questions

1. Have you been in an oppressive situation? How did it make you feel?
2. Who do you see as a great leader? What makes them great?
3. Have you been in a situation where you made the choice to forgive? What was the impact?
4. Would you give your life to protect the lives of others? Why or Why not?
5. What would happen if we choose to be true leaders and agents of change?
6. Have you ever attempted to cover up something you had done? What was the result?
7. Have you ever sought revenge? What did that accomplish?
8. Do we honestly believe that we have all the answers? Can we rationalize away Divine Intervention on our behalf that comes from humility, a trust in God?
9. Would you turn down great wealth and fame to stay true to your calling?

SPOTLIGHT ON THE ART OF GRACE

4

Leading from Behind

By: Evelyn Mosley

"Lead from the back and let others believe they are in front."

~ Nelson Mandela (19-18-2013)

Introduction

The different styles of leadership function like the song by the Stylistics, "People Make The World Go Round." Songwriter and singer Linda Creed understood that it takes all types of people to make up this world when she penned the lyrics to this song. Leadership styles are the same way. It takes various leadership styles to make a project come into fruition. This chapter will highlight a few of the leadership styles that people are more accustomed to using or seeing. From there, we will focus on my favorite style of leadership, "Lead from behind." This style of leadership exuberates confidence, respect, servitude and grace. It is inclusive as well as engaging and it promotes growth among all.

Leading with Grace

Leading with grace to some may appear to be a strange concept. For me "it is the only way." Being a leader does not mean you hover over the people you are leading. It means you give them a wide birth to be who they are, to grow, to make mistakes and, did I mention, to be who they are?"

When I was growing up in a single parent household, my mom, Gloria, was a prime example of leading with grace. She would give us choices of what she wanted us to do. For example, when it came time to decide how the dishes would be cleaned on a daily basis, she said, "you may take turns and wash dishes every 3rd day (divided between the 3 children) or you may take turns and wash dishes every 3rd week." With me being the oldest and not liking to wash dishes I opted for the later, every 3rd week with me being the last one in rotation. Needless to say that was not the first option that was started. Gloria did not like my form of leadership. Though she heard 'my' choice, mom said, "we will start with each person washing the dishes every other day starting with Evelyn (me) the oldest." I don't think I need to elaborate on how that leadership style went.

I would pay for my brother Anthony, who was the youngest child and six-years my junior to wash my dishes on the days I had to do the chore. Mom caught wind of that and put a halt to it almost as quickly as it started. As punishment, she said "each person will wash dishes for a whole week before we would switch." "Fantastic!" I thought. That was what I wanted in the first place. The only thing was the week started with me and I could not pay my brother to wash dishes for me. As you see, both options of leading with grace were played out.

<u>What is Leadership?</u>
Leadership is defined as the process of directing the behavior of others toward the accomplishment of some common objectives. It is influencing people to get things done willingly and to the standard required or above. This is information from scribd.com and 1000advices.com as well as a book, *Leadership Greatness*, by Tri Junarso.

A good leader won't rely on just one style of leadership to get the job done. They will use a variety of leadership styles to fit the needs of the team and the project goals they are working on. I don't know if I completely agree with those that say there is no good or bad leadership style, but I do agree that whatever style a person uses the effectiveness of it depends on how the person utilizes that style and probably the personality of the leader. You can have the authoritative leadership style of Hitler, but if you lead with fear people will do whatever you ask them to do whether they believe in it or not. But don't try this style of leadership. Leading people using fear, rigidity and inflexibility doesn't do well with me, or most people. I feel if a person is self-motivated and optimistic they probably need very little encouragement from a leader to get the job done. Direction or specifics of what is needed is what I find all that is needed in most cases. Here are some common leadership styles people like to choose from. Each style has its own advantages and disadvantages.

Laissez-Faire

This leader lacks direct supervision of team members and may or may not provide direct feedback on a regular basis. This person knows what is going on, but is not directly involved in it. Donna Karen (DKYN) built an international fashion empire using this style of leadership. This style of leadership is more effective when there are multiple leaders in various sites, with all trying to accomplish the same goal by a certain time frame. The leader trust others to keep their word in getting the job done while monitoring the progress of the job.

Autocratic

This is a style of leadership that allows the leader to make decisions alone without the input of others. This person has total authority and imposes their will on others. People under this style of leadership need more close supervision. They don't question the decisions of the leader. When I graduated from college my first professional job had a supervisor who practiced this style of leadership. We were always butting heads because I was always questioning her methods. Perhaps part of the issue was myself as well. Normally when a person recently graduates from college they come in with the idea that they not only want to change to world, but that the world wants to be changed and they are the one who will do the changing. Needless to say we were always bumping heads until she left after my first six months of employment. In my opinion, this style works best with people who are not really self-confident and need a lot of guidance.

Participative or Democratic

This style of leadership values the input of others but the final decision rest upon that particular leader. This is the style that I most use. It allows the team member to have a "buy in" to the project. When a person has a buy in they feel like they are an important part of the team and that their opinions matter. That is what you want your team members to feel. It will boost their

SPOTLIGHT ON THE ART OF GRACE

morale plus if any changes are needed it will help the team member to see the value in the change because they will see their contribution. This style of leadership can be challenging if a decision is needed in a short period of time

I was working on a huge married couple's retreat for my church and I mentioned that I would like each couple to have their own individual folder to place their paperwork they would be getting throughout the retreat. The team of people I was leading thought different. The sale price of the folders was ending the next day and I needed an immediate decision from the group. Since I was the leader I made the decision against their wishes to order the folders. Because of their objection I felt it best to order the folders and pay for them out of my own bank account. At our next meeting I informed the committee what I had done and they did not take that information well. They accused me of being the type of leader that if things don't go my way I would have a problem with them. At that moment they did not have a buy in with our project and they did not feel that I valued their opinions. Of course that was not how I felt and the only ways to prove that was to continue working with them on the project and not only ask for their input, but utilizing it as well. Sometimes as a leader your team will not understand your vision along with your style of leadership, but you must continue to move forward. Once the marriage retreat started, the planning committee members saw the value of the couples having their own colored folder. It was a decision I would stand by again if needed.

Transactional

This style of leadership provides rewards or punishments to team members based upon their performance results. The team leader and team members set predetermined goals. Everyone agrees to follow. The team leader has the power to review the results then train or correct team members who fall short of meeting the goals. Once the goals are accomplished, rewards such as bonuses, are given. This reminds me of when I worked for a major hotel chain. This was exactly the style of leadership they used. If we sold the required amount of hotel space we were royally awarded dinner, t-shirts and, sometimes, even a free airline ticket to a specific location. If the team fell short of the goals, everyone knew it and we just worked harder to accomplish what the managers wanted from us.

Transformational

This style depends upon high levels of communication from team leader to meet the goals. Leaders motivate the members and enhance productivity by being highly visible in the process. The leader must also be involved in the completion of the goal by looking at the big picture of the project and

SPOTLIGHT ON THE ART OF GRACE

delegating smaller tasks to the team to accomplish the goals. This leadership style reminds me of when I was the committee chair of a local Toastmasters District Conference and I had subcommittee leaders who did the actual duties that were needed. It was a great experience for me in delegating smaller tasks that made up the larger task at hand. This group of individuals was wonderful to work with and they did an awesome job of completing the task at hand. Once the conference got started the subcommittee leaders did not just limit themselves to their area, but they helped out and supported the other subcommittee leaders wherever the need manifested itself. The feedback that I received let me know that the conference was a great success!

Concept of leading from behind

Linda Hill of the Harvard Business School proposed the theory of leading from behind. When she read Nelson Mandela's autobiography, *The Long Walk Home,* published in 1995. Mr. Mandela compared leaders to shepherds directing flocks from behind.

Leading from behind is a style of leadership that I can truly say has always been my format. I don't know if that is because as a youth I was shy and I never really wanted people to know what I was doing. I would help and take the lead on things, but

I just didn't want people to know I was doing it. It was not because I was afraid of failure. I truly just did not want people to focus on me, but the entire group as a whole. We live in a world where people are saying, "Look at me! I did this. I did that. Please give me the praise and the credit!" (That is if the thing you were doing went well.) If you thought it was not going well, you would fade into the background and keep your lip tight. Or maybe you are that type of leader that not only does not fade into the background but you would be complaining all along the way about how things are being done!

In my opinion, leaders who have the need to be seen and not heard are the most dangerous type of leader. Leading from behind is graceful. It shows respect for those you are working with and it also shows maturity, confidence and, servitude.

A leader whose style is like a shepherd also takes on the role of servant. They have the ability to see the whole picture of the project. This person usually has strong ethics, integrity and is generous while setting the tone of creating a supportive atmosphere. When you lead from behind everyone feels like they play a significant role in what you are doing. The leader is normally transparent with the group pertaining to all that is needed to make the project run. In my experience people work a lot more "with you" when they have a buy in to what needs to be done. Leading from the behind allows a leader to soften their approach. They don't need to be authoritative with their people. I might add that being authoritative is not usually the best form of leadership style that yields productivity.

The Value of Leading from Behind
There is something to be said of leadership that leads from the back while you allow the others to believe they are in front. It is actually brilliant! When others think they are in front, they work harder and better. They contribute so much to the project that they don't even realize they are doing more than they probably thought they would do. They are making the entire project look good, while thinking they are making themselves look good. They come up with wonderful ideas that the team may adapt. They are enthusiastic about what they are doing and they even chip in and help others for the good of the project. If that is not servitude I don't know what is! Of course, this is a sneaky way to allow people to be servants of one another, but if it gets the job done, why make a fuss.

Leading from the back also allows for a transitional phase where the leader moves out of the way and allows others to move forward. Have you ever worked on a team project and the leader was the only one doing anything? When that happens, it is usually because that person was not effective in delegating roles. Go back to when I mentioned my mom allowing us kids to make the decision about how the dishes would be cleaned. She stepped out of the way to let me take the lead, but then she also stepped back in to show support to us by making the chore fair for not just me but for all of us. The value of leading from behind is that it allows everyone to show their style of leadership while it promotes growth in each of the participants.

The Growth Factor When You Lead From Behind

Tim Cummuta, author of *Leading the Way or Leadership from Behind*? said it best. "Leading from behind can have real important meaning if utilized properly." A good leader will not watch a team member sink in failure. Instead, they will step in and help that individual to correct their error so that not only will they succeed, but also, their self-confidence will not be shaken either. That team member grows from where they were prior to that event.

Being Uncomfortable When You Lead From The Back

Every leader experience some form of being uncomfortable when they are leading out front. You are shaping and developing others to be leaders using their own style while trying to complete the current project. You want everyone to feel confident in who they are and what they bring to the table, but you also want this project completed accurately, timely and, to the best of your ability and vision. When you are building a team, everyone must feel the autonomy power of solving problems or making situations of their own. It's like when it is time for a baby eagle to leave the nest. As it grows stronger and bigger the comfortable part of the nest becomes smaller and smaller because the parents are also removing the softer parts of the nest away as well. Eventually the eagle outgrows the comfortable nest. It must leave that nest and start its own life. That is what leading from the back will do for the other members of the team. When you are rotating to the back, which is forcing someone else to come to the front, that person becomes the leader making viable decisions for the group that others are relying upon. You have built another leader. That is servitude. That is Grace. That is Gratitude. An unknown author wrote, "Gratitude turns what we have into enough."

The Leader Who Leads From Behind Must Have a Vision

No matter where you lead from, you must have a vision for others to follow, especially when you lead from behind. You are putting others out front to achieve a common goal, the vision of the leader. You are giving them encouragement, support and, power to accomplish this objective. You also help them believe this was their vision they created on their own.

This is what I call leading from the back with respect, servitude, gratitude and grace.

Discussion Questions

1. What was your last project you lead and what style of leadership did you use?
2. Was that project successful?
3. Have you ever lead a project from behind?
4. If not would you consider that style for your future project? Why or Why Not?
5. What was the outcome compared with other styles of leadership you have used in the past?

5

Grace and Humor

By: George Hast

"Had I taken my doctor's advice and quit smoking when he advised me to, I wouldn't have lived to go to his funeral."

~ *George Burns*

That Guy

Where was the first time you were That Guy? I can remember exactly. It was in the Eighties. I had just gotten home from work, tired and hungry. My kids were using broom handles for sword fighting. As the good parent I was, I told them to stop; somebody was going to get hurt. Of course, they continued as if I wasn't there. Sure enough, several seconds later, there was the slap of wood on flesh and loud wailing. I yelled, "I told you to stop. I could see that coming." Suddenly in a blaze of light, I realized I had just become my father. I was That Guy. I also solved one of the great mysteries of my childhood. For my entire youth I could not fathom how my father could foresee the future. I thought he had some kind of gift, some mystical power. How could anyone tell what was going to happen so often? Now, I had their power. It was a perk, I guess, of becoming That Guy.

This was the first time of what would become a long pattern of becoming That Guy. It's something that happens over and over again. It is something that you must accept if you are going to prevent yourself from going completely crazy or worse. That Guy was that mean and miserable old man who was always yelling, "Hey kids get off my grass!" You must accept this with grace and humor. You must embrace it and make it part of your life so that there is one less old man yelling at the kids to get off their grass.

What is Grace and Humor?
Grace and humor is a phrase you seldom hear anymore. It's from the bygone age, a different era. In today's society with the social media of 144 characters, you are anonymous, bolder and, safe from society. You can be rude, brazen, say anything you want and, not have to worry about grace and humor, the more raw, obscene, rude and coarse the better. In our dealing with people, everybody is so busy, so wrapped up in our daily lives that nobody has grace and humor. Our presidential

candidates have campaigns using insults and name-calling and are proud if it, even boast of it. Our companies have their management run their employees with threats. No job is safe. Every employee is sure they are a phone call away from being fired. The boss doesn't even have the grace and humor to do it in person. Your job is already set up in another continent. The employee has no backing, no union protection. There is no grace and humor on the job, in the boardroom on social media and, in many cases, even in the home.

Our lives are so stressful, trying to get by on a salary that has not grown maybe in years. Our expenses, the cost of living, and the price of food have gone up every year. Our kids need the latest in everything, the latest clothes, accessories, electronics and maybe even cars. This, of course, only puts more pressure on our lives. This, of course, makes grace and humor more impossible to find at home as well as in the office.

Gosh, this is getting depressing! Let's get back to me using grace and humor when I realized I had become That Guy again. I was walking down the street to get the mail or something when I noticed some kids throwing a football around. I had this strange urge to have them throw the ball my way. That bright flash; again I had become That Guy. You see him interrupt your young as they play stickball or touch football in the street. I can remember some old guy, yelling, "Hey Kids throw the ball to me will ya?" Our game would be interrupted as we threw the ball to him. He, of course, dropped it and when he tried to throw it back to us, he could barely reach us, maybe throwing it partway. Then, we would have to chase the ball down and silently pray he didn't want us to do it again. I had become That Guy, the old man who interrupted the most important game the young kids were having in the street that day. Once you realize it's another example of That Guy, you are beginning to accept the inevitable and you are on the way to achieving grace and humor.

So why do we not have grace and humor, and more importantly, what is it? First let's look at what it is. Then, we can debate when we had it, when we lost it and even if we ever had it. We will see if we can we get it back.

Characteristics of Grace and Humor
I think a person either has grace and humor or does not have any at all. There is no middle ground. People who have it are almost Zen-like, having the poise and confidence to be almost implacable at all times. Nothing rattles them. They maintain this measured calm, through any crisis, through any situation. All the while they maintain their sense of humor, diffusing the situation with a joke or some comment to break the tension.

GRACE AND HUMOR

This is the essence at the base level. In the most intense situations, grace and humor is exuded by the person who has it through every part of their body, through any contact and in every meeting with anybody. The sense of politeness and manners is present at all times to people they are meeting as a peer or are waiting on them as a servant. Don't confuse the quality with just manners. Even in our society, some people do still have manners though it is rare--so rare that when people see it they may make a comment that this particular person has demonstrated good manners. Grace and humor is above that and it is so rare to be almost non-existent. That is precisely the reason we must work at it, look back at our lives, recognize it and endeavor it make it a common practice in all our activities.

On my road to achieving grace and humor, That Guy made another appearance. I was walking the dogs and ran into one of my neighbors. We of course discussed the weather, the sports teams that we were following, staying away from politics of course, for we were of entirely different political philosophies. Plus, I was not entirely forgiven for spoiling the neighborhood forever by putting up my Obama sign in the front lawn. We went through the length of neighbor's lawns, the noise in the neighborhood including the motorcycle that would roar down the street late a night. Suddenly, he looked at his watch, professed how late he was, and rushed off. I realized that I was That Guy, the neighbor who came down the street and talked your ear off. I remembered the dread years back when That Guy would appear, walking down the street. The way I would check back into the house pretending to forget something or to hurry into the car and pretend not to see the offending old guy. Once again I had become That Guy.

Grace and Humor as a Learning Project

I said that the quality of grace and humor was almost Zen-like, the extreme living of life in a special way. How do you get grace and humor? I think that it is acquired, not something that you are born with. I think you get it by having a life. You live life. You accept the things that are painful: losses, the defeats, and all the things that happen which are difficult to bear. To have grace and humor you must suffer some defeats. You must live through it. You must accept it, learn from it and grow from it. Once you have survived the experience and have learned the lesson, you must then put it in the past. You can't carry it as a burden to load you down and prevent you from operating successfully in the present. That past allows you to begin to have the elements of grace and humor. However, you learn from the lessons of the past; you use that knowledge to take on the trials and tribulations of the present; and you move onward. You cannot bear the burdens of the past, but the people who achieve grace and humor carry the memories of the burdens with them. It's that freedom that allows a person to be free to exhibit the qualities of grace and humor.

Identifying those with Grace and Humor

Sometimes it helps to illustrate actual people who have the quality we're talking about. The Boston Globe columnist George Frazier demonstrated this with a quality he called duende. Duende was a description of a person who had a quality from which you could not pull your attention. It wasn't beauty, but a certain star quality, a particular magnetism, a gravitas that some people have and some people don't. He would write columns listing people in the "have" category and those in the "lacking" category. People would comment, agree or in some cases disagree, but mostly he was right; some people had duende and some didn't. Grace and humor is a quality above duende. It isn't only star power. But the fact remains that some people have it and some don't. Fear not! To the people who are not gifted with innate grace and humor, this topic is an exercise to allow you to work towards attainment of some of the qualities of grace and humor. It seems in our crass society today with our dominant social media, fewer and fewer people possess the quality. It seems the exact opposite is being rewarded so it is vital that we attempt to get this quality back in our society.

SPOTLIGHT ON THE ART OF GRACE

Start with Yourself

I think, to begin, one has to start by changing themself. No one person is going to change the whole culture or our society. Nobody has the cult of personality that can do it! However, if we can adopt the grace and humor perspective for ourselves, maybe we can be an example to our family and one by one make a change. One way to start would be to identify somebody in our families that possessed grace and humor or, perhaps, has it now. We can see firsthand the traits the manners and then start to adopt them for ourselves.

In the case of my family, the one person who best defined grace and humor would be my father's sister, my Aunt Dot. She lived in Florida, moving there in the 1940's to escape a bad marriage. She and her mother moved down from Massachusetts in the early Florida Boom Years. She would come north only one in a while. When we heard Aunt Dot was making a visit, all of the children and even the adults would be elated. She was an adult that children of all ages loved. She practiced no airs; she would sit at the kid's table at Thanksgiving and, for all intents and purposes, was one of us. She would poke fun at the adults at the big table and make it seem like the place to be was at the little kids table. She had that certain quality to make those around her feel they were the most important people on earth. This was all done with an air of comedy and lack of airs that made all around her roar with laughter.

Aunt Dot would usually come with her mother; our Grandmother Nana. She was a stern product of another generation who ruled with an iron hand. She controlled, or tried to control, every aspect of all her children's lives. She was at the age when having honesty, brutal honesty, about everything, and anything was blurted out without any degree of caring what the other people felt. That is one character of That Guy. I have not seen this quality in me yet, and though I may have opinions on things, I have not reached the age where I just blurt them out anytime. That stage may come later, but back to Aunt Dot.

When Aunt Dot visited, all the relatives would come to visit. It was common for most of the people to gather in the kitchen sit around drink coffee and talk. Now as I said, Nana ruled the roost. The men, all in their 30's, 40's and, 50's, old, stern taskmasters in their own homes, would meekly submit to the rules of the old matriarch. In her presence, there was absolutely no smoking or drinking. Of course, Aunt Dot would not put up with this, at least not all the way. In the kitchen, the cigarettes would come out and the beer can would be opened and enjoyed. Aunt Dot would stand guard to keep the peace,

SPOTLIGHT ON THE ART OF GRACE

and when Nana headed to the kitchen for something, she would break out in a loud, very patriotic version of the Star Spangled Banner. This is was the signal to everybody to hide the beer and ditch the cigarettes. This would keep the day from being spoiled by her mother giving a lecture to everybody on the evils of drink. Everybody in the house was in on the act. Everybody laughed when the Star Spangled Banner broke out and Nana thought it was so very, very, patriotic.

Every time Aunt Dot came to town, all the women would go out to eat. Remember this was of a time when most wives would not go out without their husbands. No so when Aunt Dot was in town. Fiercely independent and an original free spirit she would say, "We're going out and the Old Farts can stay home." She would take all the wives, cousins, aunts and even just old friends and go out. It was a rite of passage that the females of the family would be old enough to go out with Aunt Dot. They would go out to dinner and maybe even have a drink. Imagine the women out on the town alone and even drinking. It was said by those who dared break the code of silence that the noise, laughter and, high spirits was noticed by everybody in the restaurant. Remember this was the Fifties and Sixties and, although it may now seem quaint, it was not common then. After all the gaiety, this tribe would then go home. They were usually safely home to husbands and kids by the hour of twelve. It was the Fifties and Sixties remember. Do not forget that woman's equal rights amendment was won in stages.

On the nights they did not go out, a location was picked and all the girls would gather for the card games. Bridge, or maybe Whist was favored and was taken very seriously by all but Aunt Dot. God help the poor soul who didn't lead the right card or even commit a bigger crime of trumping your partner's trash. Aunt Dot would play for a while and was as very good player. She would tire of the seriousness and again came to the nearest kid's table. There might be a game going on with the kids. Aunt Dot had showed the kids a card game she called 'O Hell.' There was of course a formal name but the kids of course loved Aunt Dot's name for it.' She would play with the kids and for all intents and purposes was one of them.

As I said, she was independent and before her time. Down in Florida she owned a store on the water in St. Petersburg that sold souvenirs. The store was very successful. Word was you did not want to tangle with her in the business world. But to the kids up north she was just Crazy Aunt Dot. When you visited her down in Florida, she would take you around the town. Still driving like a northerner: 2 speeds--fast and get out of my way. She would put on airs and say, "We're going to my property." Inland on a river, the property was a nice cottage, but to Aunt Dot it was her property. Find that Aunt Dot in your family that has some of the traits of grace and humor and learn from them and try to incorporate some of the characteristics into your life.

Recognizing Grace and Humor in Your Own Life

Back to my learning curve of grace and humor, and coming to the realization of knowing when you have become That Guy. I recently inherited a great car: A 1991 Cadillac Seville. It only has 125,000 miles on it, looks pristine and runs great. I really enjoy driving that car.

First, as I was driving down the street, I passed that same group of kids playing ball. I got the look. It dawned on me that I was That Guy--the guy driving the "ole" car in the neighborhood. I thought back and realized as a youth there was some old guy usually in shorts with black socks pulled up high on his shins driving some old car. Now in my day growing up in the sixties that car might have been 40's something or maybe even a 30's something but every area had That Guy with the old car. I had become That Guy (not in the black socks and shorts of course) but I now was That Guy in the old car. I, of course, didn't realize in my youth, as the kids don't today, that these cars were, and are now, classics. Some things are learned with age. Thank goodness!

Grace and Humor in Relationships

The area where grace and humor may help more than anywhere else may be in relationships. I was talking to my son the other day. He asked, "Do you remember such and such?" The details aren't important, they were even minor, but the important point to remember is that it was important enough to him that he remembered it. I had no recollection of the event. How would That Guy have replied? The guy with grace and humor would have said, "Tell the story again! I love the way you put things!"

There are times when being That Guy can be very destructive. My wife told me the story of when she was a little girl. Her father, although by no means rich, wanted her to go to only the best schools. He was a graduate of a small grade school in Quebec and a Junior College here in the states, but he was dreaming of Harvard or Yale for his daughter. Anyway, she was in high school and came home with pride for her a great report card. He of course looked at it and scowled, "Why didn't you get all A's?" That incident stayed with her all her life. She felt that whatever she did, whatever she accomplished she was not good enough, did not do well enough. Now, all

SPOTLIGHT ON THE ART OF GRACE

parents want their kids to succeed, all parents want their kids to go to the best schools to do well. However, knowing her father later in life, I always felt that he wanted her to go to Harvard so that he could brag to his family that his daughter had gone to that fine school. Don't be That Guy to your family. The lesson I learned from my son remembering some small detail and from my wife with her father is that small things do matter as well as not-so-small things like what my wife's father did to her.

I was driving across town the other day with a friend, and as we were going along, my friend was telling me that I either complain about the guys passing me or that guys ahead of me are going too slowly. Now remember, I am a fast east coast kind of driver. I want to get there quick as a flash. The Breaking News? Sudden recognition flashed across my brain that I was That Guy just as the kid remembers in his youth. That Guy who thinks the guy ahead of him in his lane is an idiot while the guy speaking poetic lines in the left hand lane is a moron. My reaction? A smile and a nod. That is coming to terms of your own behavior with humor and gracefully accepting it.

The most critical relationship that grace and humor may help, of course, is with your family. In today's society with all the complications of the special needs and the attempt for any society to grant full rights and privileges to all; relationships have suffered the most. That Guy is not the sole breadwinner. He is not sitting in front of the TV swilling beer waiting for the little lady to prepare his evening meal. That Guy is not sitting there in his wife beater T-shirt as she vacuums around him on the sofa. That Guy is not the guy coming home on Friday Night all liquored up while his wife waits eagerly for him in the bedroom. She may now be the primary wage earner in the family while he does the dishes--before she gets home. She may be the boss at work getting the job done while he ferries the kids to soccer practice. The dynamics have changed. Society has changed. Now, it's the responsibility for both men and women not to let That Guy, or the woman, ruin relationships for both for their entire lives. Grace and humor must be applied to these relationships so that the lives involved are better for all those involved.

Where do you start?

As I said in the beginning, grace and humor can be a learned trait. To begin the process, look to somebody in your family for traits and learn from them. Watch for the trait in people in listening. Look in the present day. But, use of the illustration of That Guy. If you look at your own life and see some of these, or maybe have some others, learn that they were your actions. Accept them with grace and humor. However, use humor to put them in the past, and use grace to learn any lessons that may be appropriate. Then, with the newly found character of grace and humor, live your lives in that manner. Enjoy life and laugh a lot!

The Good old Days

I have included a partial list of events in the past that may have been a That Guy experience. As you have seen, these experiences can happen to women, too. When you look at the past, people have a tendency to think of them as the good old days. People can remember the good in the good old days; many elements of society did not enjoy pleasant times in the good old days so the memories may be uneven. But, use the experiences to look for examples of events that may have been That Guy experiences to begin using grace and humor to change your lives.

Discussion Questions

1. Who was That Guy in your life? (Or the Aunt Dot, if you prefer.)
2. What did they say or do that you now say or do?
3. When you were young, how did you react to That Guy?
4. As an adult, did you react to That Guy with any more grace and humor than you did as a youth?

5. Have you had the opportunity to realize YOU are That Guy? How did you react?
6. How can you change your reaction to an encounter with That Guy?
7. How can you change your behavior when you are That Guy?

6

Grace in the Workplace

By: Keith Jones

When talking about Grace in the workplace, it's not about faith.
It's about how you treat other people.

~ Keith Jones

I stepped into the office, closed the door, looked at Frank and said, " Don't ever do that again!"

Frank looked at me with that look of 'I don't know what you are talking about.'

"Did you just give Andy a review and tell him he is the worst employee in the group?" I said.

Again Frank did not seem to understand where I was coming from.

I said, "You CAN'T do this to me! I have to work with these people. You told Andy he had the lowest performance review of the whole group. Now, his attitude will affect every project he is working on. Granted, Andy may have made some mistakes, but don't rub his nose in it. Your job is to be a mentor and coach, not a task master pointing out every little mistake."

I took a deep breath, waiting for what I had said to soak in. You see Frank was also my supervisor. Not sure what his reaction would be, I stood there waiting. I expected to hear either "Get out of my office!" or, "Ok, what do I do now?"

I believe when talking about grace in the workplace, it's not about faith. It's about how you treat other people.

So what should Frank have done about a low performing employee? Was it his place to inform Andy that he was the lowest, needs improvement in every category, worst of the worst employee of his group? Was it Frank's place to point out Andy's mistakes and then rub his nose in it?

So how do supervisors, or anyone in a position of leadership, lead with grace?

Frank said, "Ok, sit down. I am at least willing to listen. Where do we start?"

I sat down. "Let's start with people value."

People Value

It is important to understand that people want to be valued in their job. They want to know that they are cared for and are valued for who they are, and, not just for what they can do. They need to feel that their supervisors will listen to their ideas and thoughts on how tasks should be accomplished.

It's really that simple.

Value of an employee is so important to the health and success of an organization. The majority of people do not leave a job because of money; they leave because of their immediate supervisor. If the employee is having difficulty with their supervisor and they see no one else cares about them, they will leave.

It is the same in volunteer organizations. People don't leave organizations; they leave leaders who don't express value. If you are someone who oversees employees or volunteers, or just wants to be better at valuing others, here are a few ways to demonstrate that you value them.

<u>Caring</u>

Care for the person more than just what they can bring to your company or organization. Too many times we only look at what the person brings to the table, instead of the person in their own right with their unique gifts and talents. We are missing the best part of the person and their capabilities when we do this. The old adage of "don't judge a book by its cover" holds true here. Value the person for more than what they have done, value them for what they could do and who they are.

I remember one of the night computer operators was complaining about how the automation system was not setup to help them on that late night shift. I asked what would he do? He said that was beyond his capabilities. Really? I handed him the five-hundred-page manual and asked if he could read. He sensed a challenge. Within two months, a few questions, and a lot of testing, the night shift could almost run itself, fully automated, with more automated tracking then ever before.

When people feel that they are valued, it is amazing what they can accomplish. The end result? That person builds self-confidence as well as becoming a better employee. They will be amazed by what they can accomplish.

Constructive Feedback

Where do we learn constructive feedback? Many people have never heard of constructive feedback. When they get any feedback it is perceived as someone yelling at them no matter what the decibel level. They may have grown up being yelled at by an adult. As a leader, learning how to give constructive feedback is critical to making people feel valued. Many employees are desperate for positive feedback. They want to be recognized for their contribution. Employees add to their personal sense of value from your specific feedback. It's definitely tragic to watch an employee at their retirement party, without anyone from management, including their supervisor attending. Your actions, or non-actions, speak louder than words.

Never miss the opportunity to recognize the value people bring to the organization. How often do people assume everyone knows how important they are, if no one ever gives acknowledgement? It is important that grace-filled leadership affirms an employee's importance to the organization.

Beyond the Job

Taking an interest in an employee's world beyond the job communicates value. Not only that, but there might be a chance that an employee's interests could really add value to one's work. If a leader understands what hobbies a person has, that may lead to other opportunities at work. If you ask the personal questions, this will show you care about your people beyond the job. The little things, such as a birthday card, can be a small thing but communicate big value.

Leaders that lead with grace are always looking to improve those they lead. They do not use the position to enhance or promote themselves. It is their job to develop the leaders of tomorrow. The most powerful dynamic of value is seeing an employee promoted into a position of leadership, knowing they will continue using what you have taught them about the value of the people they will lead.

Enjoy being around people who feel valued. They can be the strongest people you will ever know.

"Frank, do you realize how the world we live in is changing? We are moving away from the strict rule-based infrastructure to a more principle based work environment."

Frank said, "What do you mean by that?"

Principles-Based Leadership

Rules are like guidelines, meant to be broken, but provide the defining edge.

We have a lot of written policies and procedures, but they are based on the past. They look at what has happened as opposed as to how to deal with the future. A ruled-based workplace is great for a weak leader. They can always point to the rules and say, "You have to follow the rules!"

"Really Frank, don't you think we have too many trivial company rules? How about the rule that says we can't have clocks on the walls of our cubical? What is that trying to prevent? Or how about no placement of objects on the top of our cubical cabinets? How about reporting our time on the time sheets every 15 minutes? Really? The best one is estimating our project time in minutes before we even start the project?"

Frank replies, "Those do sound like trivial rules. But we have to have rules."

SPOTLIGHT ON THE ART OF GRACE

"Yes Frank, but not the ones that just don't make sense," I said.

A grace-filled leader understands that some rules are necessary. No drinking on the job. No fighting, etc. Those are good rules. But get rid of the rules that are senseless. All email subject lines have a standard format. Everyone takes lunch at specific times, etc. Work with employees to identify the rules that just don't make sense. Remove the rules that have a negative impact and get in the way of those core values that are meant to help deliver the product to the customers. In turn, employees will be able to be more focused on doing their job than worrying about following the rules. It seems that management gets so hung up on making rules that it makes it hard for employees to ever do any productive work!

A leader who fosters a principled work environment provides guidelines that empower people to make good decisions. It provides flexibility and creativity in finding solutions.

To help develop a principled-centered environment, it is important to effectively communicate the core values of the organization. These values are used as guidelines under which the business operates and achieves the goals for the business.

Principles, that support the core values, will have teams achieving amazing results.

A grace-filled leader plays fair; treats one another with respect; and, tells the truth. They value the contributions of the team; respect their own limitations as well as those of others; and, know that they ride on the shoulders of those who came before them. They applaud great work and they celebrate the successes. They know when to work hard and when to work harder.

A strong, grace-filled leader learns how to laugh at themselves, embraces a challenge, and engages the employees to help meet that challenge. They partner with their customers and lead their team. They never take credit for someone else's work, and they will do what they say they will do. They are clear about team expectations, expecting every member to have honesty, respect, and integrity.

In today's complex, demanding work environment, how does grace help us transform a rule-based workplace into one that is governed by principles? Defining a few those principles may help guide that grace-filled leader to accomplish just such a task.

SPOTLIGHT ON THE ART OF GRACE

I could tell Frank was curious by the look on his face. "Principles you say? Just what kind of principles are we talking about?" said Frank.

"Frank, here are a few principles I am talking about."

Mind Your Manners

The way you treat others and how they treat you, your personal interactions, are vital to your success as a leader. The simple things you do create the relationships between you, your colleagues and employees.

Write emails as if they were memorandums, not as if you were posting on Facebook. Memorandums may be a lost art since we are so used to sending emails to our friends about our latest adventures. Emails in the work environment should have a purpose, either be informative, or have an action associated with them.

Be prepared for meetings. After all the training I have watched managers go through, I am still baffled that an agenda is never provided ahead of time. We are called to meetings not knowing why we are there or what will be discussed. It's hard to prepare without knowing ahead of time. Prepare an agenda and distribute it ahead of time.

Respect the time of your colleagues. When you don't show up on time, it shows you don't care for your colleagues. Remember caring for others is a core value. If you have to cancel provide as much notice as you can and reschedule as soon as possible.

Summarize meetings and any action items for everyone. Make sure every person at a meeting knows the reason they are attending. Writing down what happened at the meetings prevents the attendees acting like it never happened? Always summarize meetings with action items and distribute the summary to all. Make sure information filters down to those that need to know.

Your body language speaks louder than words. Improve your ability to read the nonverbal clues of others. Keep a friendly smile in your voice as well as on your face. Friendly body language such as open arms shows you are open to new ideas. Crossed arms signals a negative attitude with a bored or defensive stance. Courtesy words, like please, thank you and, how may I help, will go a long way to treating employees with grace.

Minding your manners generates graceful behavior when greeting people, facilitating introductions, and breaking the ice.

SPOTLIGHT ON THE ART OF GRACE

Engaging people by making eye contact goes a long way making them understand they are the focus of your attention.

Be Present

How do you create an environment that is constructive and open to your ideas? When others feel understood and a part of the solution to a problem they are more likely to be engaged. There are behaviors more subtly than body language to create such an environment.

Be an active listener that gives affirmative nods at appropriate times. Respond in a timely manner to employees and colleagues. Be aware of others reaction to you and your comments. Avoid body language that may indicate you are distracted. Tapping a pencil, playing with paper clips, or clicking a pen shows you are bored and disengaged. Share ideas and give consideration to others ideas. Be sure to apply these behaviors to everyone, your employees and your colleagues. To be present, you must give full attention with your eyes, words, and body language and speak in terms your employees can understand.

How do you know you are using these behaviors? You participate actively in meetings by demonstrating active listening techniques, and give timely and frequent updates to employees. Ask questions to identify employees' needs using friendly and engaging language.

One question to ask yourself, has your behavior changed since you became a leader?

Be Positive

A grace-filled leader understands projecting negative emotions will have a ripple affect on the attitude and productivity of the employees they supervise. Remember to recognize the work of others. Encourage trust and build confidence rather than blame others. Mistakes are inevitable, but leaders must expect that employees learn from their mistakes.

Always use positive language that focuses on the future. You must be open to new ideas that allow you to seek options to solve tough problems. Look on mistakes as opportunities to learn. Set goals and work to achieve them, but remember to be flexible.

Being positive in dealing with your employees fosters a healthy environment for people to flourish.

Create a Team

Create an environment that facilitates the growth of energetic, productive teams that produce quality results. Gather your team for activities outside of work. Challenge the team to interact spontaneously and share ideas. Facilitate work areas to encourage collaboration among employees. Teams are functioning well when all members are positively engaged, and producing quality products in a timely manner.

Sweat the Simple Stuff

The simple stuff takes many forms.

Tell the truth. I always say I tell the truth so I don't have to keep track of the lies I have told. Exaggeration may have impressed the girls on the playground, but you are not in school anymore.

Be sure to say thanks. We don't thank people for the little things anymore. It's a good habit to maintain.

Respond to phone calls, emails promptly. That may call for better organization on your part. This is especially true when your inbox has hundreds of emails and you can't find the one you need.

Keep appointments with your employees when you schedule meetings. And don't forget to send out the agenda ahead of time!

Rediscover Silence

We are never taught to listen. Oh yes, we have been told to shut up, but not to listen. Obtaining feedback from your employees will require you to learn how to listen. Your employees will need to be in a comfortable environment to feel they can give you constructive feedback. It will be your job to be open to new ideas and receptive to concepts you may not be familiar with.

Another side to discovering silence is the work environment your employees are given. If your employees are in an open, no wall workspace, there may be a lot of interruptions and distractions. Some people do not work well in these conditions. Some employees will enjoy and be more productive in a place that eliminates the side distractions of people walking or talking around them. Giving people sufficient workspace with access to a computer, will allow them be much more productive.

Remember to listen carefully, don't interrupt, and invite your employees to contribute.

With these few principles, a grace-filled leader will foster a principled work environment that will empower people to make the decisions worthy of their time, effort, and skill to produce amazing solutions to problems they once thought were impossible.

"Frank, now that we have covered the value of people and the principled-work environment, how do we make this a safe place to fail?"

<u>Safe Place to Fail</u>
Although some businesses are starting to understand the concept of the value of failure in the workplace, nowhere is the fear of failure more intense then in the competitive world of business. There is a whole set of polices, processes, and practices geared to deal with people and projects that fail in the workplace. Employees are in fear of making a mistake that can mean losing a bonus, a promotion, or even a job. The fear of losing a job could even drive employees into illegal actions. While there are times when losing the job may be a legal or safety necessity, not every situation should face such an unnecessary consequence.

A grace-filled leader, new to an organization, may find them in a culture where the employees are terrified of failure. The employees may have been trained to see unsuccessful projects as personal failures. It is important to understand that this type of culture will hinder the creative thinking necessary for healthy employees, and a healthy work environment.

To bring grace to the work place is to create a culture of intelligent risk. A project that fails due to a half-hearted, careless effort with poor results is unacceptable. But a project that is well thought out, planned with a collaborative effort of everyone on the team, fails, it should be used as a learning experience. This type of learning experience builds confidence for future success. Leaders need to push people to reach beyond a simplistic, traditional definition of failure. Failure is the compliment of success, because without facing the risk of failure, success would never be achieved.

"Frank, do you see how Andy will now spend more time on trying to prevent mistakes instead of being focused on his work and creating solutions?" I asked.

"I am starting to understand some of the work I need to do to make our team function better", said Frank.

Move Beyond Success and Failure

To move beyond success and failure requires management to stay engaged with the process. With any failure and even success it is important to examine the results to determine how this information can be used for the betterment of the organization. Leaders need to question success and failures in the same way. Both need to be approached to distinguish if even the failures moved us closer to our goals. Simple illuminating questions help bring the spotlight on the process.

- Was the project a collaborative process?
- Was the project carefully organized, or was it haphazardly run?
- Could the failure have been prevented through more research or consultation?
- Were mistakes made repeatedly?
- What did you learn from this failure or success that will help you, or the organization in the future?

Taking a different perspective and raising such questions, a leader will begin to treat success and failure more alike for the betterment of all.

A grace-filled leader may find it difficult to treat both failure and success the same, but this understanding will lead to the ability to see the larger picture of how both are interrelated.

Get Engaged

Grace-filled leaders are more engaged with their employees. The focus should be on increasing the organizations' intellectual capital, the experience, knowledge, and creativity of the workforce. These leaders take an interest in their employees' projects, to better understand the work, and discover the meaning to the individual. They are in a position to see the work in a larger context and help relate the significance to the organization.

A collaborative effort by the leader expresses support for the project. Conversations are more about what can be learned from the experience than success or failure. Nothing does more for productivity, morale, and employee retention.

Listening is more central to the process than talking. By leaders being actively involved in the discussions of projects shows an interest that no incentive can match. The obvious appreciation shown by a leader's interest and enthusiasm produces creative acts on the part of the employees.

SPOTLIGHT ON THE ART OF GRACE

Frank said, "Ok, I understand why I should practice active listening. Tell me more."

Don't Penalize, Analyze

Leading with grace means to interpret more than evaluate. Sometimes it is better to analyze, then to penalize or praise. If you penalize your employees, they won't take risks. They will be to busy trying to prevent mistakes from happening. If you praise too much, employees don't think you are authentic. Too many compliments and employees will think it is a joke. Recipients may feel manipulated.

Instead, ask questions, give feedback, and show interest. This shows more interest in the employees work and is more appreciated. Genuine engagement takes more time. It demands that the supervisor use the skills of listening, to facilitate the skill of analyzing an employees' work.

Earn Empathy

We all must learn that failure is not a disgrace. We must analyze each failure to find the cause. We must learn to fail intelligently. Failures are just practice shots at success. The key is to create a risk friendly environment. A grace-filled leader must be willing to share their failures. Convey to the employees that failures will be tolerated. Use failure to move forward toward success.

For example, think of Abraham Lincoln and all the failures he had in business and in political life before becoming President. Looking at his life, didn't the failures he endured shape his decisions and actions as President? If someone like this can be so revered as a great person, can't we all learn from failure?

Far from revealing weakness by admitting mistakes, a leader shows their self-confidence. A blunder admitted earns empathy. Leaders who do not cover up their errors reveal themselves as human. They show that they are still learning to be better. They become people who others can identify with and admire.

"Obviously I made a mistake with Andy," Frank said. "What can I do now?"

Collaborate to Innovate
Sharing information may not be comfortable for people working in an environment built on personal competition. Show me a competitive work environment where employees are awarded for performance and I will show you people with a desire to win and not solve problems.

A grace-filled leader will have to abandon the traditional ideas about personal competition. Employees will need to feel they can share information freely to help innovation flourish. A simple example would be to have a common group of employees share when they each will be out of the office. Sometime it is the simple things that bring employees together. Employees sharing the simple things will break down the barriers of sharing all information. Realizing sharing information should not be intimidating or threating to their jobs, employees will start to share ideas that increase solutions the company needs.

The main objective of collaborating among employees is to share information. How can a company function effectively without all the employees being on the same page? Innovation comes from within the information explored, researched, and discovered by the employees of a future-minded company.

Communication technologies have allowed a different type of collaboration to assist employees to share more information than before. Email is just a start to establishing electronic suggestion boxes, chat rooms, news groups, and joint document preparation as a way to further allow the spread of ideas and information vital to everyone's success.

A grace-filled leader will need to encourage collaboration between employees to help them feel a part of the greater organization.

"Frank, Andy needs to feel more a part of this work group and the company," I said.

Give the Green Light

Has your organization ever created an open suggestion box for the whole company? Some of the best ideas for improvement come from the people doing the work at the lowest level within the company. Proposals would be submitted to a central committee trained to assess ideas and review as to how they would benefit the employees and the company. Employees will surprise management by how innovative they can be because they may have never been had the opportunity to express their ideas.

A grace-filled leader will realize a good idea is a good idea. Giving employees the chance to share their ideas in a place where they know they have an honest chance of being heard will build courage. Courage will give employees the confidence to contribute to the innovations that drive the company. These people will feel ownership and more a part of the company, making them long term employees. Given the green light, employees will no longer think in terms of success or failure, but instead in terms of learning and experience.

Final Words

"Frank, we have covered a lot of ground on leadership. Caring, constructive feedback and beyond the job are all part of understanding the value of people. Principled-based leadership changes the focus of the organization from focusing on rules to guiding the employees to make better decisions. Following a few simple definitions of principles, such as minding your manners, being present, and being positive help to build better teams. Sweating the simple stuff is just that simple. While rediscovering silence and making the workplace a safe place to fail helps the company or organization move beyond the successes and failures. Grace-filled leaders are more engaged, understand how to analyze and earn the empathy of their employees. Employees who are given the green light to collaborate in the workplace will be more innovative."

"I hope you now understand why I came in your office in the first place. I want what's best for our team. I need your help Frank for us to achieve our best."

Frank sat there for a moment, and said, "Just where did all this come from?"

"Frank, you have always valued my work and have listened to my opinion. Besides, I have spent more than forty years in the workforce, and I just wanted to help you, so you could help us."

"Alright, now get out of my office, while I try to digest what you've said and figure out how to approach Andy to make him a better employee." said Frank. As I stood up and turned towards the door, Frank gazed out his window thinking about 'Grace in the Workplace'.

<u>Discussion Questions</u>
1. So what should Frank's approach to Andy be now?
2. What does 'Grace in the Workplace' look like to you?
3. How would a Principled-Based work environment help your company?
4. How has failure made you a better person?
5. How will grace make you a better leader?

SPOTLIGHT ON THE ART OF GRACE

7

Thankfulness

By: Charles W. "Chip" Mackenzie, Ph.D.

"Along my journey I have learned that
the more *thankful* I am, the more
I have to be *thankful* for."

Saved from www.cumberlandheights.org

How do you view your life? Have you been lucky? Are you a self-made person? I am in my third marriage. I am in a power wheelchair. While I have a Ph.D. in Biochemistry and in computer science education, I recognize that many factors and people have made my successful life possible. I have no reason to believe that the future won't be similarly blessed with grace.

My Life Framework

In the winter of 1952, I stayed home from school one day because I was sick. We had a housekeeper watching me that day. I had permission to go to my parent's bed during the day. When I got out of my bed to go to their bedroom, I couldn't stand up, so I crawled to their bedroom. I do not remember any distress. That evening the doctor came to my home and I was taken by ambulance to Sacramento County Hospital, where a spinal tap confirmed that I had polio. I was 6 years old.

I was thankful that I had not ended up in an iron lung or even unable to walk at all. In the hospital, I listened to Roy Rogers and Hop-along Cassidy on the radio. One day, they put my bed next to a patient in an iron long. I am thankful that the nurses noticed the distress of the iron lung patient after I played with the knobs on the iron lung. A sign was posted on the iron lung warning everyone not to place the little boy next to it. I was in the hospital for 9 months and came home with long leg braces and crutches.

As I continued to strengthen over the next few years, I threw away the braces and crutches. After polio destroys many nerve connections, amazingly the remaining nerves branch out to reconnect with muscles that no longer have a nerve connection.

This return of strength primes polio survivors like me to believe that anything is possible with hard work. People with polio marry and have kids at normal rates. They are more likely to have a college education and are less likely to have Alzheimer's disease. I figured that I couldn't dig ditches, so I had to use my brain. Unfortunately, my parents (my father in particular) never complimented me, believing that they had to be hard on me to prepare me for my future. I left for college without a good sense of my potential.

The Role of Education

In my second year of college, an ailing fraternity approached me. They had only 6 members and not enough students were pledging their fraternity in the regular fraternity pledge process. The fraternity resorted to going through the dorms looking for members. I joined the fraternity, Alpha Kappa Lambda. It was the best thing I could have done! We had the highest fraternity GPA at my college. Our dinners were formal and manners were polished. These manners serve me well to this day.

When we had parties, I had a good opportunity to get a date. One or two fraternity brothers stayed upstairs and played records (remember them?) with Rock 'n' Roll artists like The Yardbirds, The Doors, and The Beatles and love ballads sung by Andy Williams, Ed Ames and Claudine Longet. I later recorded the music on a 7½-inch reel-to-reel tape player, so everybody could be downstairs at the party. My future wife went with me to many of those fraternity parties.

I was secretary of the fraternity for 3 years. It was not a prestigious position but it meant that I was part of the leadership. The year after I graduated, the fraternity had grown to 50 members. The experience with leadership has been repeated in many groups over the years. What a blessing!

Back then everything was falling into place. I graduated college, married my college sweetheart, and went to graduate school in Biochemistry at the University of Southern California. To get a medical school position, one or more years of post-graduate study was required after getting a Ph.D. I found a very interesting researcher at the University of Minnesota, who offered me a position. With my wife 8 months pregnant, we moved from Southern California to Minneapolis. My first time driving in snow was going through Iowa on the way from California to Minneapolis. I noticed I was fishtailing going over the bridges. I did not stop until I got to my new home. I had no idea of the many challenges awaiting me.

Brrr!

The morning my daughter was born in early December, it was 8° F. I knew it would get colder than that but I had never experienced that low of a temperature before. By the following winter, my wife was cross-country skiing across Minneapolis along the Minnetonka Creek. The snowplows were out early in the morning and I didn't miss a day of work while in Minneapolis. My coldest morning in Minneapolis was a night when I worked until 4 a.m. On my way home I passed a jogger along Mississippi River. The temperature was -25° F; the wind chill was -50° F. Those experiences left me with the attitude that winter is just another season. Those were good years despite breaking my ankle one year at the St. Paul Winter Ice Carnival!

Then my dreams began to fray. After two years in the first lab, I moved to another lab for two more years of research. After four years in Minneapolis, I had no new publications and no job offers. I was not willing to give up my dream yet, so I accepted yet another postdoctoral position at the University of Nebraska Medical School and moved to Omaha, Nebraska.

My Research Career

I was still chasing the dream of a medical school faculty position and got one in the Pharmacology Department at

University of Nebraska Medical School. I had a knack for writing grant requests — getting grants from the American Heart Association, the American Lung Association and the National Institutes of Health. I had ten publications, three in the top biochemistry journal, The Journal of Biological Chemistry. During this time my son was born.

My social skills were inadequate for the type of collaboration that was needed to build a lab with graduate students and postdoctoral researchers at a medical school. I had a few connections with other researchers around the country (several of whom have won Nobel Prizes). The Pharmacology Department chairman did not support me for tenure, much to my disappointment. I had to admit that my heart was no longer in the academic realm.

Computers!!!

While continuing my research career, I purchased my first computer: an Apple II+ with 48k of RAM. Soon I found that the only thing I was doing outside of work (and often inside of work) was learning about computers. I studied computer science at the University of Nebraska at Omaha. At the age of 40, having failed to get tenure at the medical center, I decided to switch careers to software development. I developed and marketed my own software, named RefBase. Refbase stored references related to people's research and created the bibliography automatically from a manuscript. After 4 years with no net profit, I switched to computer consulting to make a living. I supported software, which generated tests for textbooks for Delta Software on the Apple II. This was later expanded to include the Macintosh and IBM versions of the test generation software. I also created software that collected weather reports for a weather company. Twenty-five years ago, weather reports were typed in by hand. The program the weather company used was picking up less than 75% of the reported weather reports. I was able to revise the program so that more than 95% of the weather reports were successfully picked up.

Post-Polio Syndrome

I was beginning to have trouble physically. I knew something was going on but didn't know what it was. During this time, my mother sent me an article out of a Southern California newspaper that talked about an Omaha woman named Nancy Baldwin Carter. Nancy was publicizing something called Post-Polio Syndrome. Nancy was furious when her doctors had passed her on to a psychiatrist for her complaints of weakness and fatigue. Nancy started a publicity campaign to get the word out about Post-Polio Syndrome. I had the opportunity to appear on local television to answer questions about Post-Polio

Syndrome. I thought I had done a pretty good job but, when I got home, my daughter (a teenager) accused me of staring at the beautiful news anchor. My daughter had no comment on what I had said. I was named vice-chairman when the group incorporated as the Nebraska Polio Survivors Association. Ours was the first statewide post-polio group in the nation. I was instrumental in organizing the first Nebraska post-polio conference. For nearly a decade, I got speakers for the monthly Omaha meetings and assisted with the monthly newsletter (which went out to more than 2500 people at its peak).

While the post-polio and business struggles were going on, my wife of 23 years decided it was time to part, after our daughter finished her college applications. I had been working at home for the preceding 7 years. I was terrified I would be alone the rest of my life. I could not have more wrong! My first wife kindly found me a bedroom to rent in the home of a divorced man, who could not afford both his home and his child support payments. He rented me one bedroom and later added another roommate in the basement.

Moving Onward with my Life

I cared for my first wife a great deal more than I had let on. I was determined not to make that mistake again. Grace followed me everywhere I went. I made a promise to myself that I would thank everyone who did something that I considered special. One example was Jackie, the woman I danced with for my first dance after separating from my first wife. I sat for nearly two hours, trying not to cry because my wife was not with me. I finally asked Jackie to dance. I danced very close to her. She was intuitive and did not take offense at the closeness. I called her the next day and thanked her for the dance. Another example of grace was when my stepfather lost one of his sons to cancer. I wrote him a letter spelling out the special role he had played in my life. It was the only thing I could think of to give him and it was greatly appreciated. This evolved into complimenting people, even people I did not know, when I observed something special about them.

As a single person, I was out 4-5 nights a week to a variety of single groups plus church every Sunday. I decided that I really did not know what I was doing in relationships. That left me open to some people whom I would never have considered earlier in my life, including my second wife.

I became a leader of numerous single groups including the Omaha Parents without Partners. I found there were many people who really cared for other people, especially at church single groups. While not as secure as when I was married, I found that I was less lonely single. I had learned to verbalize my life in stories before I left my first wife. This skill allowed me to easily get to know many people. I learned that I had a charisma that showed up when I was out with other people, as evidenced by the girl who called me one day and asked me how I could always be so positive. That was news to me! By the time I got remarried 3 years later, I had met more than 300 people and invited more than 200 of them to Roxie and my wedding.

I went to several divorce recovery groups, hoping to be able to move on more quickly. The sessions were very educational, especially the one where I spotted my ex-wife also in the audience. I turned around, went down another aisle and introduced myself to someone new. Eventually, I learned that recovery was different for each person, although I did get some guidelines. One important guideline was that it takes about one year of recovery to heal from 5 years of marriage.

I went to single dances in my wheelchair. Then I would hop up, grab one or two canes and go out to dance. The wheelchair greatly assisted me in remaining active even when I was exhausted.

As I got married only three years after I separated from my first wife after 23 years of marriage, I was really not fully ready to remarry. We married when we did because Roxie's children needed her at home, not running around with me every night.

Remarriage at Age 50

My second marriage was to someone quite different from my first wife. Roxie was a bakery manager when I met her, with no college education. She was incredibly creative and enthusiastic! She would eventually get a BS in psychology and a Master of Social Work. Our counselor warned her that I tended to be co-dependent. She took on the challenge of straightening me out. She challenged me from then on when something I said or tried to do did not feel right. The modern phrase "It's all good" applies as we both grew immeasurably in our marriage.

Fig. 1. Chip and Roxie taken by movie theater manager in Winterset, IA

Parenting was something that I never thought I was any good at. While my first wife and I did not co-parent well, Roxie and I co-parented very well. There was something special in our parenting of Roxie's children. We eventually ended up handling her children as follows: I could criticize my kids and compliment hers. She could criticize her kids and compliment mine. It took some time for Roxie to become the fine parent she ended up being. Within a few years, we would talk about all decisions relating to her kids. Then she would decide what to do. Ultimately, she had the last word on what we did with her kids.

One time when my son was visiting, he asked Roxie to tell me that I didn't need to keep telling him the stories, which had served as a teaching tool when he was growing up.

Another Change in Perspective
Roxie and I had a special song (For all We Know by the Carpenters), a special animal (the otter), and a special romantic memory (the covered bridge). The special song reflected the realization that nothing was guaranteed in life with the line "Love may grow for all we know". The otter was chosen as our special animal after Roxie observed them at the zoo for a psychology assignment. The otters love to play and were to remind us to remain playful. We have more than a dozen otters

(stuffed, statues, pictures) collected through the years. The covered bridge came from the fact that I proposed on a covered bridge, after watching the movie "Bridges of Madison County" in Winterset, IA (where it was filmed).

Fig. 2. Covered Bridge Picture from Chip and Roxie's Wedding Invitation

We have numerous covered bridge items including a tapestry and numerous pictures. A picture of a covered bridge that we drew was on our wedding invitations. If you look closely inside of the bridge you will find our initials: CM+RS.

Over the years I changed my perspectives on my life to realize how many things I had to be thankful for. I remember how sad I was when my first wife told me that she had hoped to be married for a lifetime, but she had changed her mind. In the case of Roxie and I, cancer ended our marriage when Roxie was only 55. I had become aware of how grace had touched my life in so many ways. While Roxie died young, the kids and I are doing well. While I miss her, her life and her parenting were clearly blessings. She was easily the most mentally energetic person I have ever met. She had opinions on everything and everyone. She always complained that I never listened to her. That would have been foolish as she was right more than 90% of the time. From her perspective, not agreeing with her 100% of the time was not listening.

I learned a number of important grace lessons from her including:

1. Be prepared to change direction in life immediately when the opportunities arise.
2. Manners are not needed as long as you can put yourself in the other person's place.
3. People die but the love lives on.

I thought Roxie had so much to offer the world. It did not make sense that she should be the one to die young. My focus is to carry the essence of Roxie in my own life. She had encouraged me to remarry and the week before she died she said, "I know I love you but I don't understand why. We are so different!" She left me believing that I could love again.

Back to the Singles World

I decided to "grieve" for a year after Roxie's passing. Each month during that time, I went to a grief group and read a book on losing a partner to death. It was shocking how many of the scenarios detailed in the books applied. It was more than just the stages of grief spelled out by Dr. Elisabeth Kübler-Ross. I had always handled the bills in my marriages, but now I found it difficult to make financial decisions. I was fortunate to be part of a worship group at church that gave me good connections and grace as I healed.

On my birthday following Roxie's death, I realized that I had to celebrate alone. I decided to go to Hooters. I started talking with my waitress, telling her of my journey. Much to my surprise, all of the other waitresses came to my table, one and two at a time, to hear my stories. As these were relatively young women, I had to frame the stories in a way that was meaningful to them. I could not have asked for a better birthday present! Their kindness was just the grace I needed.

Grace next surprised me on the following Valentine's Day, which was a Sunday. I was introducing a song, which had the word love in the title, as part of leading a worship service. As I got ready to introduce the song, I realized that I still had Roxie's love. My voice failed me as I said: "I no longer have a partner but I still have love". Many people in the congregation smiled, showing they understood what I had tried to say.

I drove from Nebraska to California and back the following summer, to visit my relatives and college fraternity brothers. I wanted to go to prove that I could choose to go by myself even though I had no partner to help with the driving.

I was still awed by how much Roxie had meant to me so I decided to write a book about her (titled "Once Upon an Otter" available on Amazon). I also decided to sign up with an Omaha matchmaker, Omaha Love. The first date was appalled by my liberal political views. The others they matched match me to during the first year were blown away by my verbal energy. Omaha Love invited me in for a little "counseling" to better connect me with my dates. In particular, they told me to not tell everything about myself on that first date. The counselor explained that the information should be shared in chunks, like chicken tenders. Mary Ellen was the first match after that.

The matchmaker's computer system was malfunctioning so I did not know that they had scheduled a date for me. When Mary Ellen called to confirm (having expected me to do that), I told her that I had not been notified of the date but could still meet her for dinner as planned. We met at an Italian restaurant. I started to tell a story then stopped because I was not supposed to tell her everything the first night. I ended up telling her half of at least 30 stories over a 3-hour period. About half way through, I mentioned about liking touch. We ended up holding hands for the last hour and a half. When we talked about it later, she said that I reached out for her hand but I could have sworn that she reached out for mine.

The matchmaker matched her with another man the following week at the same restaurant. She realized how much more fun she had had with me the previous week. She called the matchmaker and told her not to send her anyone else while she checked me out. I took her to a movie on our next date and invited her to accompany me on a 10-day trip to visit my daughter in Charlotte, NC and my stepdaughter in Orlando, FL. She agreed to go with me after another week, but her daughter wanted to meet me first. We met with her daughter and granddaughter for dinner. I felt like I was being given the third degree. After about an hour, Mary Ellen's daughter suddenly flashed the biggest smile at me and I knew I had passed the test. I was so tired by the time I left the restaurant that I didn't realize that the person in the parking lot having trouble starting her car was Mary Ellen. Whoops!

Four weeks after we met, we left on our trip. She drove the first part of the trip. I knew she had chronic fatigue syndrome, so I figured I would just keep talking to ensure that she would stay alert while driving. Every day she told me another story about her previous husbands (there had been three). On the third day of the trip, I turned to her (she was still driving) and told her that I was a better man than she had been married to before. I have met two of her ex-husbands and I am, in fact, a better man.

I had been telling her that people were the most important things in my life. On the eighth day, we were driving at dusk in a light sprinkle when she missed the turn for the freeway. When she hit the curb, she blew out the right front tire and even put big dents in the rim. She pulled over to the side of the road, crossed her arms and turned to me and waited to be chewed out. I smiled at her and said that were both OK so it wasn't a problem. What an opportunity to make a point on the man I was!

We got married a little less than a year after our first date. I thought that it might be fun to get married in my home. She agreed. Only later did I realize that she would be inviting 120 people! More than 100 people signed the guest register. My stepfather, a Disciples of Christ minister, flew out from California to perform the wedding along with my mother and sister. We had two big tents in the backyard with tables and chairs.

I recently talked to a widower who asked if I felt like I was betraying my spouse because I moved on. I told him that remarriage allowed me to contribute to another family, as my kids from my first marriage and step kids from my second marriage were doing well.

We are approaching our fourth anniversary and I have to admit life is good. Mary Ellen said she wanted to take care of me. As a man, that sounded great. She is a woman of her word. We both have ongoing challenges since we are both past 65. All of our children are doing well. Something always hurts (usually one thing at a time) but we have the grace to handle the challenges with love, patience, and acceptance. I figure that, as long as people think we are younger than we are, we can't be doing too badly.

Looking Back

I remember many people who really weren't looking forward to any changes in their lives after their 40's. I didn't want to have that happen to me. It hasn't!

When I look back over my life, I see many things to be thankful for. While there have been losses, there has always been gains and grace. I have a can-do attitude that has grown stronger over the years. I am thankful that I have had wives with whom to share more than 40 years of my life. Having taken so many college courses (and received two degrees) through the years, I feel I can learn almost anything. Now it is nice to be able to choose not to learn sometimes.

While I am aging every day, I am learning more all the time. I now keep track of all the current news worldwide and am getting involved in some political campaigns. I do not know what tomorrow will bring, but I know I will have rich experiences and am thankful just to be alive. My desired ending scenario is described in the following quote by Hunter S. Thompson:

> "Life is not a journey to the grave with the intention of arriving safely in a pretty and well-preserved body, but rather to skid in broadside,

THANKFULNESS

thoroughly used up, totally worn out, and loudly proclaiming - WOW – WHAT A RIDE!!"

Discussion Questions

1. How have you been blessed in your life? What role has grace played?
2. What do you stand to lose (or gain) by recognition of how grace has played a role in your life?
3. I was surprised that my wife would be willing to consider a fourth marriage after all the things she had been through. What has grace opened the doors to in your life?
4. If you see someone in a wheelchair, will the stories in this chapter come to mind as to how you think about them?
5. What factors make your life successful?
6. What role has education played in your life?
7. How can you become more thankful for what you have?

8

Breaking the Mold

By: Christine Jones

"It takes but one positive thought when given a chance to survive and thrive to overpower an entire army of negative thoughts."

~ Robert H. Schuller

Meet an Introvert

"Hi. My name is Christine."

Do you know what it took for me to say that? Fear filled me from my toes to my nose! Having been an introvert ALL of my life, I had finally decided to do something about it. At age fifty-something, with some coaxing, I stepped into a room full of STRANGERS! Filled with fear, a burning stomach, and sweaty palms, the above line was how I introduced myself.

No, I had not entered Introverts Anonymous. (At least not exactly.) This was a group of people that meet regularly to learn and practice speaking and leadership skills. Have you heard of Toastmasters International? Ralph C. Smedley started the organization over 90 years ago. No, they do not sit around making toast or drinking toasts. (Okay, one project does allow you to practice making a celebratory toast.) There are an abundance of speaking projects from basic skills to storytelling to technical presentations to managerial communication. My thought was that this would be a safe place for me.

The first project you present is called an Ice Breaker Speech. You basically introduce yourself. By doing this, you get to take that first step of talking about a familiar subject, you, while the audience gets to know you and your speaking style.

My story goes like this.

"I was born the fourth of five children. Growing up in central Nebraska, my Mother would constantly criticize me. I had trouble feeling like anything I ever did was 'good enough' to please her. That is really what a child lives to do after all. As a result, I became afraid to try new things. Meeting people

BREAKING THE MOLD

became absolutely traumatic for me. I would literally break into tears and hide behind my Mom or Dad. It would later result in teasing from my siblings. Being the fourth allowed them to be able to also bully me when parents were not within earshot. It would take until we were all past our twenties to allow grace to work through what their bullying had done to me. Now, you have a better understanding of why I am introverted.

I also have a fair amount of spunkiness that has served me well as I became an adult. By the time I was a High School Senior, I was determined to go to college and get a good job away from my siblings. I became the first in my family to graduate from college, 45 miles away from home, then, move to the Big City of Omaha, 180 miles from home. (Each was an extremely stressful step for this introvert.) There I began my professional career. Yes, that was also where this tall, handsome man that I had met in college was living and working. A year after graduating college, I married him! We have been married for over 37 years now. While he HAS been a big help, I have remained introverted.

Our marriage was not without challenges. Because of my job, auditing many of his peers, I bottled up work issues. It took perseverance to identify the cause of our strife. Grace and strong faith brought us to a better place! When we determined my career was a severe detriment to our happiness, I became a housewife. (I shudder to think what I would have missed had I not given up that job! You see my family expected me to "use my degree" rather than "throw it all away.") We came to this decision because of the importance of our marriage vows to each of us. Quitting our marriage was never an option for either of us. We then had a daughter and a son that kept me busy.

As my children grew, I volunteered in their classrooms and at Sunday school, attended many a dance practice and recital, was a Cub Scout Den Leader, attended Track and Cross Country meets, fitted marching band uniforms, as well as attending marching band competitions and performances. (I may have forgotten an event or two in my list!) This all happened while I addressed personal medical issues. Being generous with grace, these two children helped keep our family strong. My children learned that while what they do may not be perfect, they do a darn good job making their Mom happy! They are now in their twenties and building their own futures.

My life has molded me into this introvert that stands before you today."

What about the Mold?

Why did I say that I had not exactly joined Introverts Anonymous? It took me a while to realize that a great many people in Toastmasters are also introverts! Oh. My. Goodness. Could this organization help me break the mold?? There are times that I really wish to be less introverted.

In order to break the mold, first I need you to understand what I mean by a mold. Dictionary.com says a mold is "a hollow form or matrix for giving a particular shape to something in a molten or plastic state." That makes me think of those little green army guys! You pour in liquid green plastic, let it cool, and pop out various stiff characters. I am happy to remind you that they are just an example we will use for our discussion. Imagine all of the different characters you could create. Like humans, no two would be alike. They are just not flexible!

We next need to understand who created our mold. You have been told about my childhood as well as my career having an affect my marriage. Early family life, faith, society, career choices, and the early years of my marriage all led me to FEEL that I had little value to contribute to the environment around me. That is what I THOUGHT my mold was. My character was more like a sad person hiding under an army tent so well that you could only see the tent.

The process of defining and resolving the challenges in my marriage included making a list of things I liked about myself while my husband made a list of things he liked about me. Because of the negatives my Mother constantly identified, I had perfected becoming my own worst enemy. That meant that I could not find anything that I liked about myself but plenty that I did not like. By the grace of my husband, I began to learn to squash the negatives and reshape my mold with my better attributes. What I did not see in my mold was my perseverance, determination, and my true abilities. What I learned through this process is that when we look at ourselves through the eyes and grace of someone else, we can reshape our own mold into what we really are and want to be.

We are Connected

I am not writing this to tell you my life story. Rather, I feel a very strong need to connect with YOU. How about taking a few minutes here to look at you? What do YOU see molding

BREAKING THE MOLD

you? Write down three things in your notes. Now ask someone to list three things that they like about you. Are there items on the lists that you want to make more prominent? Is there something you wish was less prominent? What would your green army man resemble? I encourage you to write about this in your notes.

Good News About Our Molds

Could you use some good news about your mold? No, I cannot wait until later to tell you this. You CAN change it!!! How? Go back to the beginning of this chapter and really read the quote. Think about what it says! That mold is not made of stone or some other immovable material.

It IS made up of the changing environment in which you currently live. That is to say that green army men in an office environment will be shaped by the organized lifestyle of the city that surrounds them. Perhaps, they live in a war environment that thrives on being in the trenches. If these two were to switch places, neither would feel like they belong. What makes them good in one place can leave them feeling terribly inadequate elsewhere. They can choose to be uncomfortable or they can go find their comfortable location.

I repeat. You CAN break your mold! By looking honestly at ourselves, we can find ways to better adapt to wherever we find ourselves. We do not need to be stiff green toy army characters in order to survive and thrive. I hear you saying, "That is what she thinks."

Read along here and let me tell you my thoughts about this. First, make a quick analysis. Spending a great deal of time on this becomes over-analyzing. Stop over-analyzing! Yes, listing possible options and results is a good exercise. While, you may not find your answer on the lists you make, you have done something worthwhile. The process is a good way to eliminate obviously inappropriate choices. The more important aspect of this exercise is that you are beginning to use your brain to employ problem-solving skills! You need to set limits on this process because too much of life will pass you by while you are analyzing. My suggestion is to get busy picking a potential option that can at least get you started, then, go work on it. Spending time and energy on the work is much more beneficial than spending it analyzing!

Small steps are perfect! When you learned to walk, you had more control if your pace was slow and steady. Keep that same focus here. (Note: stiff green army men cannot take ANY step without help. Let me help you for just a bit.) As you work, you need to set checkpoints that allow you to merely make a Yes or No decision as to whether or not to continue your current direction. While 'Yes' decisions are self-explanatory (keep going), 'No' decisions will require you to stop to do a bit of an evaluation. Look at the 'Why Factors' before you abandon this path. This includes identifying if you want to quit because of some fear that is holding you back from a breakthrough. Decide if you want to quit because it takes too much effort for very little reward. If the reward is truly worth it, then face the fear!

Face Fear!

Let's spend some time facing fear. Did you know that fear can range from fear of failing to fear of succeeding?!?! Are you afraid that someone will not approve of what you are doing? It is time to get to the bottom of what fear has a grip on you. Get out your notes and spend some time honestly putting on paper what you fear and why. ***Do not skip this!*** Yes, you have fear. No matter how little or how much you have, you need to tackle this. NOW! You can have more than one type of fear gripping

SPOTLIGHT ON THE ART OF GRACE

you. This is where you need to be a strong green army character. Identify your enemy/enemies! Prepare for attack!!! Write it down. Look at it. Now, write down what you will gain by getting past your fear(s). No matter how small you expect that gain to be, in actuality it will be much, much more. Write your plan of attack.

I know that was hard. Yes, it was very necessary to put you through that. If you have been truly honest with yourself, you will soon see that you are about to make a really big breakthrough. How big of a breakthrough will depend on what you decide to do with your new knowledge about yourself.

Are you going to let that fear hold you back? Or are you going to find a way to use it to propel yourself forward? In reality, I found myself taking a few steps then stopping to waver. Asking myself if I wanted to go back or forward, I would renew my resolve to go forward. I can take my cue from those green army characters who do not like to retreat. As long as you keep taking even tiny steps forward, you are doing great! Holding your ground is just as important. I sincerely mean that. Just thinking about what doors could be about to open for you literally makes me want to jump for joy! You deserve to see what awaits you!! (Just do not leave me yet. Take a deep breath and get ready. There is more to learn.)

Learn!

Remember back where I told you that it took until we were past our twenties for my siblings and I to work through the bullying? That was quite the moment. I was doing the hosting of Christmas with family that was now scattered across several states. I had planned the meals, bought the groceries and cleaned my humble home in preparation. Mom and my oldest sister came in with even more groceries as well as the usual "you are not doing it right attitude." Rudely, they began to push my preparations aside. I absolutely lost all control! There was no turning back. The battle was happening! Strong words were exchanged and many tears flowed; but then came that magic meaningful moment of understanding.

Yes, there remained a great deal of tension as we managed to work our way through the holiday, but the understanding that resulted in a moment of grace brought my family closer together when I had feared that it would rip us apart. I learned that understanding what molded me as well as facing my fears became a necessity in order to see who I was in that moment.

SPOTLIGHT ON THE ART OF GRACE

(It also became the moment that I realized that I had control of my mold.)

My Mom was able to finally tell me that she treated me that Not Good Enough way intentionally! WHY?!?! Her thinking was to get me to try harder because she saw more potential in me than I was using. We came to the conclusion that she was not using the best tactics to encourage me. Thankfully, we were able to have several more years together to learn to share a more positive relationship. Taken by cancer much too soon, she was not there as I raised my children. The grace that I gained from this revealing lesson did allow me to raise them to try harder while they know that they are loved and do many things that please me.

As for my siblings, we continue to work on our relationships. At times, I still feel like a bit of a Black Sheep. That is, I question if I fit in with my other four siblings. Those moments have become much less frequent as the decades go by because we have learned to not bully each other. Instead, we gracefully acknowledge the good things we see in each other. There remains a healthy dose of teasing, too. We have learned to live in the moment and enjoy what time we have together. We are glad that none of us are inflexible green army characters.

Things could have been different if my mold had been different. I have learned to just be thankful that we have learned about the impact we have on each other. We now change the mold by having a more conscious sensitivity in our current relationships. Even though we may be physically scattered from Virginia to Minnesota to Nebraska, we have built strong bonds that keep us emotionally close.

<u>Make Changes!</u>

What about you? Make some notes about what shaped your childhood. Note what you have changed. Was it for the better? Do you see something that you would like to work on improving? Even if you have lost the people that helped mold you, for better or for worse, you CAN make changes today. Just understanding what they shaped in you can go a long way. You have the power to continue living as you have or to make changes to reveal the real you. It is time for us to break the green army character molds and build our own molds.

I mentioned that my family felt that I threw away my degree when I gave up my career to become a Housewife. Both my husband and I disagree. No one can take away the life experience I had as I spent four years earning the money to pay my way through college, the classes, the people I met, nor the

SPOTLIGHT ON THE ART OF GRACE

independence I developed. My degree in Computer Science has helped me understand the value of technology in today's world. The real benefit to our marriage is that I have an understanding of my husband's career allowing me to be supportive of him and the challenges he faces. That alone tells me that I have not thrown away my degree. I have just used it differently than my family's expectations!

One of the most important lessons that I have gained is that I continue to learn! I treat each day like a new page in a book. As you read a book, each page tells your more of the story. Right now, you are reading part of my life book. What would I read about you? Each day, my green army character also gets molded just a bit different to reflect me better.

Since my life is not complete, I need to examine each new page to learn what will happen next in my life. It has been quite busy the last few weeks! Let me explain.

As part of a brainstorming session, this group decided to collaborate on this book. My right knee has been deteriorating over the last few years. Of course, during a visit to my Orthopedist about two weeks into this project, he decided it was time to prepare for surgery. While one would think five weeks of preparation would be more than enough time, it went very fast. I was doing physical therapy three times a week, going to the gym daily, and doing exercises at home twice a day. This was just to become physically ready. It was also necessary to prepare my home as I would need to function using a walker. Believe me, using a walker was challenging! I quickly found my time to write was severely limited. Oh, the grace I have been given by this group! They told me that I could write as I recover. When pain medication forced me to nap frequently between working on physical therapy, it became harder than expected to work on writing or editing. Keep in mind that this group set an ambitious schedule for the completion of this book. Since I was part of setting the schedule, I have tended to feel very responsible if the dates are not met.

What changes did we make? Two weeks after surgery, we met to see how we were doing. I had managed to read every one of the submitted chapters making notes for each author. We spent part of that meeting getting others to read someone else's chapter to give a second opinion on my thoughts. What did I learn? People value MY opinion!!! While there were a few additional suggestions dealing with some long sentences, my notes were deemed appropriate and encouraging. That has been a real morale booster. Their support told me that I needed to keep on keeping on with my recovery and this project!

Yes, there were a few chapters lagging behind in progress. That is still a good lesson, too. Not everyone works at the same rate. Others also have responsibilities, fears, and health issues. All of these have an impact on our abilities. The schedule provided me a window that let me alternate between editing and writing. Yes, I was uncomfortable at not being ahead of the others in my writing. At the same time my discomfort helped to propel me!

Discomfort

Before I tell you how this happened, I want you to make some more of your own notes. Write down what discomfort is to you. Then make a list of what discomforts you right now. Be sure to look at emotional as well as physical aspects. For me, I felt guilty that my chapter was not finished before everyone else's. I also faced physical discomfort as I healed from surgery. Pain medication reduced my physical discomfort but also reduced my ability to function, as I would like. It has also been a discomfort to get the other writers to finish their work.

Now that you can identify discomfort, we need to look at how we can use it to propel ourselves forward. Think of a child having an all-out temper tantrum. They are most uncomfortable with something, or the lack of getting something. What are they doing with their energy? Usually, they are screaming, stomping/kicking and crying. Since you are an adult, you would like to act a bit differently, right? While we have used green army men in our discussion, we will use our brains and not violence to solve this.

Quick! Before you lose any energy, write down ways YOU could use this energy. Do you see the lesson? Use or Lose the Energy of Discomfort! Rather than sit and stew about my situation, I opt to look at what needs done next and get busy doing it to the best of my current ability. "Success IS failure turned inside out." This is a line from an anonymously written yet inspiring poem, Don't Quit. (You can go look it up on the Internet. Just do it after we finish here!)

To me, discomfort is failure staring me in the face. After all that I learned from my Mother, you can be sure that I will not let failure win! She was right that I have more potential. Today, I have learned to see the potential for myself. At long last, I can reevaluate my 'Yes/No' decision process discussed earlier. It gives me energy to move forward. As you can tell, this book has been completed. Decisions were made to mentor each other as needed to see chapters to completion. The significance of each chapter meant that we would hold publication the few extra days it took to get every chapter finished. While discomforting at the time, I am comfortable with what you now hold.

<u>Grace</u>

Another component of all of my lessons are grace. As the Editor of this collaboration, I spent some time reading the definitions of grace. Among them are mercy; kindness; goodwill; favor; pardon; moral strength; honor and, willingness. While there are other definitions, these are the ones with which I identify in my chapter. All of them are possible for me because of my Faith. What about you? Get your notes out, look up Grace in your favorite dictionary source, and note how many of the definitions relate to your life.

Here is your next challenge. How do you give grace to others? We have spent quite a bit of this chapter looking at ways of receiving grace. Do you know that in giving grace, you also receive grace? When you are kind to someone, they are more likely to be kind to you. You can make your own notes about how this happens with the other definitions from above. (Do not be fearful here. The answers ARE within you!) It is amazing to feel the energy that happens when you experience receiving because you gave. If you have not been aware of this, make an intentional effort to give grace to someone just to enjoy the experience. Keep practicing. Like when you learned to walk, it took quite a bit of practice to become proficient. Write yourself notes about how you progress. This will help you develop awareness and savor the joy of the experience.

<u>Bottom Line</u>

As we near the end of our time together, I want you to see the bottom line of this material. I began with introducing myself as an introvert who joined Toastmasters. While it may not be Introverts Anonymous, I soon learned that many introverts are members. Whether or not you may be introverted, I encourage you to check into a Toastmasters Club. You will find a great place to learn leadership and speaking skills that you can use every day. Throughout this chapter, I have identified lessons that I learned along the way. As I continue to turn the pages of my life, I will continue to learn. The green army toys were used to remind us that neither you nor I are stiff and unable to be altered. Having looked at elements of life that mold us, we spent some time facing fear and how to attack it to make ourselves into who we want to become.

I do have days when the world seems to have more people than I care to face. Yet, because I have learned more about what has molded me, I can take a deep breath; make that 'Yes' decision to face them; and, because of my faith, overcome my fears to face them anyway. The grace that has come to me because I do this is much more than I could ever fathom. While I may not always take the time now to write out notes like I have asked you to do, I do stop and spend time reflecting to allow myself to make my 'Yes/No' decision before moving forward. Taking the time to write things down as you learn this process gives you tangible material to look back upon to see how you have changed.

For me, writing out this chapter has allowed me to learn much more about myself. It has given me the opportunity to reevaluate my fears and practice anew the skills I use to reevaluate my mold. My new knee is settling into working nicely and the muscles continue their healing and strengthening. Why does that matter? If my body can heal itself following surgery, I can be confident that I can mold myself into the person that I really want to be as I take on this world. If I were to describe my green army character now, it would be standing tall, smiling and much more confident than the one hiding under that tent. What am I most confident about now? I am confident that YOU have the ability to look at yourself in a new way that will help you become the real you!

Here is my challenge to you. Re-read and digest every chapter in this book. Make notes. Spend a great deal of time reflecting on the questions that are within the chapters. Sit down with someone else who reads this book and talk aloud about what you learn about yourself. Then, make YOUR plan to mold yourself into who you really want to be. There are pages left in your book of life. Break out of that green army character mold and write those pages your way! Conquer your fears and receive the grace you deserve.

Discussion Questions

1. What are three key lessons that you have learned in your life?

2. What three things does someone like about you? Are you willing to make them a focal point of who you really are?

3. What did your original green army character resemble? What do you want your new character look like?!

4. What changes are you willing to make to become the real you?

5. Find someone to mentor you as you carry out your attack on those fears that you identified.

6. Highlight any of the lessons identified in this chapter. Is there any that you need to learn for yourself? Discuss your concerns.

7. What different lessons have you learned? What can others learn from your lessons?

9

Turning Life Experiences Into Learning Experiences

By: Mark Fegan

Das, was uns nicht umbringt, macht uns stärker.

(That, which does not kill us, makes us stronger.)

~ Friedrich Nietzsche

Over the years, I've attended a number of workshops where various speakers have attempted to prepare us to "go out and do great things." During my years as a Secondary Mathematics Teacher, the "great thing" was to inspire our students to learn. There was also an undercurrent; the speaker was also attempting to get us charged up, to inspire us to be

SPOTLIGHT ON THE ART OF GRACE

great teachers. One thing I noticed: every speaker filled his or her presentation with personal, inspirational stories.

I was left wondering; where did they get their stories? Is there a book somewhere filled with personal stories? Why did I have to live such an uninspiring life?

At this point you may be wondering, "Just who is writing this chapter?" To fill in a bit, I'm a mature adult who has enjoyed two careers and also enjoys two avocations. My first career, Mathematics and Computer Science Teacher, started when I graduated from college in 1975 and continued for twenty years. My first position: Junior High Mathematics teacher. My final position: Assistant Professor of Mathematics. My second career, starting in 1996, is in Software Development. I am still active as a software developer as I write this. I also have two avocations: music and public speaking. I am a member of Toastmasters International and three community concert bands. As a Toastmaster, I have written and presented over 100 public speeches over the past 8 years; as a musician, I currently play in approximately 15 concerts each year. These avocations, together with my family, help keep me sane in an otherwise stressful world.

One additional background fact: I tend to be somewhat introverted. In particular, I don't generally go looking for projects; rather I let them find me. That includes writing this chapter. My original thought: "What do I have to offer?" Then the editor and I talked. This chapter is the result.

A Flashback to a Simpler Time

It was a long time ago, when I had just turned eight years old. I joined the Cub Scouts. My family was living in Cass Lake, Minnesota. Cass Lake is a wide spot on the Mississippi River, 100 miles or so down stream from the headwaters.

In those days there were two big events in the Cub Scout year, the Blue and Gold Banquet and the Pine Wood Derby.

That spring, I was presented with my Pine Wood Derby car; actually it was a kit consisting of a block of wood, two wooden axles, four nails and four plastic wheels. The kit also included directions with a set of plans. Each Cub Scout was expected to build a car for the race.

I immediately set to work. Following the plans, I crafted my racecar; it looked like the classic Soap Box Derby car. Narrow in front but expanding back to the cockpit and tapering to a rounded aft. The wheels stood out from the body on axles.

I was proud of that car. I just knew it was a winner. After all, I built it myself.

Unfortunately, I also played with the car a bit. Or, a bit too much. One of the front wheels, the right one, came off. Already showing signs of my male heritage at a young age, I fixed it myself by wrapping a rubber band around the front axle. The wheel reattached, the car was ready to run.

Race day was a beautiful spring morning for Northern Minnesota; most likely it was cool and a bit breezy. I grabbed my car and jumped into the family Chevy with my parents, my brothers and my sister. My Dad drove us to the race site, a picnic area on the shores of Cass Lake and I entered my car into the Cass Lake Cub Scouts Pine Wood Derby.

When my name was called, I carried my racer to the starting gate and placed it on the track. I knew it was going to win. Part of me expected the other boys to scratch their cars from the race and declare me the winner.

The starter raised the starting gate...

Four Memories

I didn't appreciate it when I was sitting through all those inspirational workshops, but this childhood memory, one of the sharpest memories I have retained all these years, could form the basis for an inspirational story. We all have memories, experiences we have had and have learned from. In this chapter I'll share a few of my memories, memories I have turned into inspirational stories, and provide you with some ideas on how to turn your Life Experiences into Learning Experiences.

My life experiences:

1. The Pine Wood Derby race when I was eight years old

2. My year as a Junior High Mathematics Teacher when I was 22 years old

3. A lesson learned from Mark Twain, Tom Sawyer and a Tomato Garden

4. My experience becoming an actor when I was 53 years old

Over the years, I have morphed each of these experiences into short inspirational speeches; speeches I have presented several times for audiences. Reflecting on these and other memories has also allowed me to adopt a more grace filled approach to life. I have learned to find grace and positivity in even the most difficult and disappointing situations. Finding grace in such situations has helped me to keep a positive outlook, enabling me to learn from trying times and then move forward with life.

A Side Trip into Mathematics, Physics and a Sand Box

George Polya was a Hungarian Mathematician who immigrated to the United States after the outbreak of World War II. While at Stanford University, he wrote the book on Problem Solving entitled *How to Solve It* (Princeton University Press, 1945). Based on his study of successful problem solvers, he proposed a four-step heuristic for Problem Solving: Understand the Problem; Plan your Solution; Carry out your Plan; Review and Extend your Results. His final step is sometimes written as "Look Back and Reflect"; I like to think of it as "Learning from Your Experiences". Some organizations include this concept as the "Lessons Learned" phase of a project.

One misconception many people have is that you can't learn from a failure. In fact, learning has made many critical advances in science and technology from a seeming failure.

On a personal level, reflection allows you to see the benefit in the most difficult of situations. Of course it may require time before you can learn from your experience; taking time to reflect on your experience will allow you the time to react with grace rather than anger as you learn from your apparent failure.

In the late nineteenth century, physicists were convinced that that light could not travel through a vacuum. As a result, they postulated the existence of a substance they called *luminiferous aether*, a substance that filled the vacuum of space but was essentially transparent to motions by ordinary matter. In 1887, American physicists Albert A. Michelson and Edward W. Morley conducted an experiment designed to measure the effects of the *aether* on the speed of light. The experiment failed. With its failure physicists were forced to conclude that *luminiferous aether* did not exist and that light could, in fact, travel through a vacuum. This failed experiment became one of the seminal events in Physics and resulted in a complete rethinking of the discipline.

My purpose here is not to provide a lesson in physics; rather it is to point out the need to *Look Back and Reflect* on your life experiences. Learn from your experiences, good or bad, as you

SPOTLIGHT ON THE ART OF GRACE

progress on your journey through life. Learn to be graceful as you react to your experience.

A few weeks ago, as I write this, my eldest brother, Dave, and his wife visited my family. (In one of those odd coincidences, in the mid 1970's, Dave and his family lived in the same town as my wife and I have lived the past 20 years.) As we were talking, Dave related an experience he had with the family car, a trunk full of sand and two young law enforcement agents. His story was extremely funny and vividly told. I could easily picture the entire event. But I was left wondering: "What did you learn from this experience?"

As you continue on your life's journey, I challenge you to look back at, and learn from, your life experiences. Find the lesson and grace that each experience is trying to teach you.

Back to the Derby

At this point your may be asking, "How do I do that?" "How do I learn from my Experiences?" "How do I change Life Experiences into Learning Experiences?"

TURNING LIFE EXPERIENCES INTO LEARNING EXPERIENCES

Let's return to the Pine Wood Derby for a minute. When we left, my car, the winning car I had built myself, didn't just lose the race; it failed to even start the race. Imagine what it was like to be the eight year old who built the car. Does he quit Cub Scouts? Does he slink away in shame? Does he learn anything from this experience? There surely can't be any grace, on the surface at least, in of this humiliating experience.

Did I quit Cub Scouts after that race? No! Did I slink away in shame? I don't know. In fact, I don't recall my reaction that day.

Later that summer, my family moved from northern Minnesota to a small town near Milwaukee, Wisconsin. I joined the local Cub Scout pack and completed the program including winning the "Arrow of Light", the highest award then available in Cub Scouts. I truly believe that losing that race allowed me to approach Cub Scouts and later life ready to accept defeat with grace and to move on to the next experience.

Did I learn anything else from the experience? I believe I did, although it took years for me to really voice what I learned.

SPOTLIGHT ON THE ART OF GRACE

Remember the car? I built that car. Win or lose, that was my car I was racing. Here's what I learned:

1. I should have glued the nail into the wooden axle rather than using a rubber band.

2. It really is OK to lose a race. After all, not everybody can finish first in the race. The important thing is to do your best. Afterward, accept the result with grace, learn from the experience, and move on with life.

3. What was important in this case was building the car; win or lose, that was my car. I made it myself!

In short, I learned that the work I put into creating that Pine Wood Derby racer was more important than winning the race or even, as it turned out, starting the race. The work I put into the racer, the journey I was on up to the starting line made a seeming failure into a success.

That experience and the lesson it taught me was so important I still remember it after more than fifty years. That's a life experience; what it taught me was a learning experience.

The Challenge To You

Here's the challenge to you: If you want to want to turn life experiences into learning experiences, you need to approach life with a learning mind set. You need to:

TURNING LIFE EXPERIENCES INTO LEARNING EXPERIENCES

- Take a reflective approach to life. After an experience, look back and ask yourself what the experience taught you. What did you learn from the experience? How can you apply that newly gained insight to your life?

- Treat failure as a learning experience. Ask yourself what the failure means. Did you make a mistake you can avoid or are your assumptions incorrect? Above all, don't dwell on the failure; learn from it and move on, but move on with grace, no anger, and no regrets, just grace.

Many of us take perceived failure poorly. The challenge is to handle failure with grace. I don't mean to accept failure and quit; on the contrary, a failure should prompt you to look back and learn from that experience. This will lead to success over the long run.

It's really up to you. You can live in the past, or you can learn from your experiences and use your life lessons to guide you into the future.

Was it a Failure?

I graduated from college May of 1975 and went out to make my place in the world as a Secondary Mathematics teacher.

SPOTLIGHT ON THE ART OF GRACE

After an extensive search and several interviews, I accepted a position as a Junior High Mathematics teacher in a small school district in western Minnesota. As one of several rookie teachers that year, I started with nothing: no friends, no apartment, no food, and no money. My girl friend of two years transferred to a college in another state. I ended up sharing a trailer house with another rookie teacher.

As it turned out, the school I joined was in turmoil; half of the secondary faculty was new that year and most of new teachers graduated from college that spring. Part way through the year our English Teacher quit; he left school on Friday afternoon and never returned. We also had two High School Art teachers that year. I completed the entire year although I resigned my position before the end of the school year. (That's an odd thing about teaching contracts; you can resign and complete the year. You basically quit later, but resigning looks better on your record than simply quitting.)

It was a rough year, both personally and professionally. As I said, near the end of the year I decided to resign my position and actually decided to quit teaching. That was rough. It was the end of my dream. At the end of the year, I packed my belongings and slipped out of town.

Another Side Trip into Mathematics

I am a classically trained Mathematician! I have undergraduate and graduate degrees in Mathematics and was pursuing a doctoral degree, also in Mathematics, when I changed career paths in 1996.

"Mathematician" literally means "Student of Mathematics" and I was a rather good student of mathematics. As a student of Mathematics, my teachers led me on an exploration of Mathematics. In the classical approach, the teacher leads the student in a rediscovery of the subject whether it is Algebra, Geometry, or one of the more advanced Mathematical disciplines. Once past basic arithmetic and algebraic manipulations, the student is encouraged to discover and prove various theorems relating to the discipline.

There is, of course, much more to the study of Mathematics. There are a couple of core points:

- Mathematics is a very abstract study. As you study Mathematics, you need not concern yourself with applications; Mathematicians don't concern themselves with applications. Applications are left to lesser fields such as Physics, Engineering and Economics.

- You should never solve the same problems twice! You may build on one problem to solve another, presumably more difficult, problem; whatever you do, don't solve the same problem twice.

That second point may represent the major flaw in a Mathematical Mind Set. Imagine if Michael Jordan had never taken another shot after he made his first layup. Much of our journey through life consists of solving the same problem again and again and yet once again.

Notably missing from my Mathematical Training was a serious study of problem solving. Yes, we solved many problems in the many mathematical disciplines but Polya's work never entered into the equation. Critically, although we were taught many techniques for solving Mathematical problems, the importance of Polya's fourth step, **Review and Extend your Results,** was never mentioned. As a result, although I was well versed in solving Mathematical problems, I wasn't always very good at solving real life problems.

Back to Junior High

As I noted previously, my first year as a teacher was also almost my last. Why didn't I just give up? A quick answer is that I had invested several years of my life learning to be a teacher; I simply wasn't going to throw that investment out the window (and quit).

Going into that first year, I was well trained in the mechanics of teaching. I could create lesson plans, craft lessons and deliver those lessons to the students. What was missing from my education was the mechanics of being a teacher. These involve such things as long term planning, managing group dynamics, community relations, etc. As painful as that first year was, both personally and professionally, I was able to learn from that experience; learn how to be a teacher. (I've frequently heard experienced teacher say, "I learned more my first year as a teacher than in my four years of college!")

That year taught me the importance of preparation and the importance of perseverance. It taught me to learn from experiences, both good and bad. It taught me to apply what I learned as I continued through life. It also taught me to be graceful in defeat, to find Life's Lesson in the defeat. Be graceful and move on. All in all, not bad lessons to learn.

I also learned not to burn any bridges. Dealing with disappointment and failure with grace is difficult especially

SPOTLIGHT ON THE ART OF GRACE

when you want to curse those you believe have wronged you. You never know where or how your actions and attitudes will impact your future. Being graceful in defeat now may lead to stronger ties later. In any event, if you react ungraciously the impact later will be negative and will likely affect you long after the incident has passed.

Did I apply those lessons learned? After that first year as a Junior High teacher, I went to work in the garment industry for a year. I then returned to teaching in the fall of 1977. Among the recommendations that helped me gain that next position was the Principal from my first school. (I am sure glad that I had not burned the bridge to him!)

I also believe that first year, as painful as the experience was, helped me to gracefully accept the worst that life could throw at me allowing me to take stock of the situation and move on.

Over my years as a teacher, I continued to learn from my experiences and refine my craft. Without the ability to look back at my experiences, analyze those experiences, learn from those experiences, and, most critically, to apply those lessons, I would have finished my teaching career in 1976 rather than 1996.

A Mark Twain Experience

Most Americans have either read Mark Twain's *The Adventures of Tom Sawyer* or have seen one of the movie adaptations of Twain's novel. In perhaps the most famous scene from the story, Tom is tasked by his Aunt Polly to white wash her fence. What Tom does is to white wash several of the neighborhood children. By convincing them it is fun to white wash the fence, Tom extracts payment from boys for the privilege of doing his work!

Quite honestly, I didn't believe this story reflected any reasonable reality.

A few years back, we decided to build a garden spot in our back yard. To be fair about it, this wasn't the first garden we attempted although we were hoping we would finally succeed. The driving force was my wife's desire to make some salsa, from scratch, using homegrown tomatoes, peppers and onions.

SPOTLIGHT ON THE ART OF GRACE

To make the task manageable, we would keep the garden small and build it above ground level. This actually involved two steps. First we used retaining wall blocks to build the elevated container for the garden and then we filled it in with dirt.

Finally, the big day arrived, the *Day of the Dirt*. Minding my own business, I arrived home from a hard day at the office and attempted to turn into our driveway. There, looking much bigger than life, was the dirt!

I was confronted with a heap of dirt, 5 cubic yards of dirt, hundreds of pounds of dirt. The new garden was only about 30 feet away, standing between the dirt and its destiny as a garden? Our house! Armed only with a shovel, and aided by a wheel borrow, I started to move the dirt the long way (of course) around the house, through our back yard and eventually into the new garden.

Then a minor miracle occurred: after I had moved a couple wheel barrow loads of dirt, several of the neighborhood children showed up on our driveway wanting to help. They brought shovels, wagons, and other tools to do the job. No bribes changed hands; they simply wanted to help move my dirt.

After planting the seeds and watching the plants grow, we really enjoyed that Salsa!

Looking back on that evening three thoughts really standout:

1. A child views life as a series of experiences/adventures and doesn't expect anything more than the experience in return.

2. Children are gradually trained out of that viewpoint; life in America teaches we should always be paid for our efforts.

3. As a result, our children grow up to become teenagers, and then adults, who expect to be paid for every contribution they make to the community.

The Lesson

Very simply, our neighborhood children saw an opportunity to make a gift to our family; a very valuable gift, the gift of helping me complete the strenuous, and rather boring, job of changing that pile of dirt into a garden for growing salsa.

Approach life as an adventure. Be willing to contribute to your community without any expectation of payment for your labors. Remember that the real joy in any gift is not in receiving; it is in the giving; the true value of any gift is measured by what the giver brings to the table. Take time to be gracious about gifts, both giving and receiving.

As I noted earlier, music is one of my avocations. I started playing the cornet when I was in grade school and continue to do so all these years later. I play for fun, but also because it allows me to provide a service to the community including helping to provide music at various community events in and around our hometown. I always make a point of graciously accepting all complements, usually responding, "Thank you. It was a pleasure to be here."

In summary, if you approach life the way our neighborhood children did, you'll look for chances to contribute to your community. If the children had waited for me to ask for their help, I would likely still have that pile of dirt on my driveway. Also remember, whether giving or receiving, be gracious. Being gracious will make all involved feel better.

Who wants to be an Actor?

Have you ever been caught between desire and fear; wanting the positives from the experience but so fearful you are unable

TURNING LIFE EXPERIENCES INTO
LEARNING EXPERIENCES

to say yes or no to the experience? This seems to be especially true for many people and the reportedly Number One fear: Public Speaking.

After I quit teaching in 1996, I accepted a position as a "Software Engineer" and relocated our family to one of the Omaha suburbs. As part of the transition, I joined the local Methodist Church. We moved in August; the next spring, as Easter approached, I learned that the Maundy Thursday service featured a Living Last Supper commemorating that point in the Last Supper when Jesus says, "One of you will betray me." The presentation was both inspiring and thought provoking.

After attending the service for several years, I started to believe I should take the part of one of the twelve in the reenactment.

My chance came in 2009 when the director, a good friend of mine, asked me to join the cast. What could be simpler, the director wanting to cast me and I wanting to be in the Cast?

Unfortunately, although I was a teacher for twenty years and was very comfortable leading classes, I had a fear of standing up in front of an audience and giving a formal speech. Of

SPOTLIGHT ON THE ART OF GRACE

course, this included delivering a memorized speech as part of a play. In short, I was afraid to accept the challenge, join the cast and perform in public but I also didn't want to let my friend down.

I did what any reasonably sane person would do when confronted with such a dilemma; I procrastinated. That's right, I put off making a decision and skipped the first rehearsal. I was hoping the whole thing would simply go away!

Eventually my friend, the director, tracked me down and I turned down the part. I also immediately regretted that decision and came to realize the result was a lose-lose situation. I not only surrendered to my fear, I let my friend down.

When you find yourself in a situation like this, you essentially have two choices: you can either retreat from the challenge or you can elect to face and (attempt to) overcome the obstacle.

My obstacle was a fear of public speaking. Considering my background as a teacher, this fear was a bit ironic. My choice was to face and defeat this fear. To do so, I needed to do something about my comfort zone. I needed to move public speaking into my comfort zone!

Getting out of Your Comfort Zone

Everyone lives in a sweet spot called the comfort zone. Your comfort zone is where you feel well comfortable. For me, my comfort zone did not include public speaking; interestingly enough getting up in front of a class to teach was firmly in my comfort zone.

I frequently hear advice: "You need to get out of your comfort zone." The problem I have with this advice is simple: leaving your comfort zone makes you uncomfortable. This tends to have two results. First, you jump right back into your comfort zone, and, perhaps more critically, you are less likely to try a new experience.

I have found it much more practical to stretch the boundaries of my comfort zone. Try new experiences a little at a time. You'll find yourself enjoying new experiences and yet you'll be safely in your comfort zone.

Becoming an Actor, Scene 2

I decided to face and defeat my fear. To help me, I joined a Toastmasters International. Toastmasters International is an organization that specializes in helping its members become better communicators. You join a local club, which provides support and encouragement as you work to achieve your communication goals. Within two months of joining, I stood up in front of my Toastmasters club and delivered my first prepared speech; a speech I had written and practiced.

As I recall that night, I was rather uncomfortable; yes I was worried about standing up and speaking, but I was more concerned about how the club members would react to my speech.

I need not have worried. The club members provided a warm reception and showed their appreciation for my effort. I received a very helpful evaluation of my speech. In the process, my comfort zone grew a bit and it became easier for me to stand up and talk to other groups.

The program I followed involved writing and presenting 10 speeches, each speech project working on a different aspect of public speaking. After each presentation I received immediate feedback on my presentation. Eventually, I was also to provide feedback to other speakers in the club. In all, I gained three valuable skills, writing a coherent speech, delivering that speech, and accepting criticism that enabled me to become a better speaker. As a bonus, I also learned how to listen to and evaluate another person's presentation. I became more graceful in my approach to receiving an evaluation, even a critical evaluation. I also learned to give an evaluation with grace in a manner that provided assistance to the speaker.

Almost as an afterthought, I became more comfortable with speaking; my comfort zone continued to grow with each speech I presented.

Finally, after presenting several speeches, I was once again asked to become a disciple for the Living Last Supper service and this time, without hesitation, I accepted the role. That was in 2011 and I have been a member of the cast every year since.

It is a bit of a cliché, but there are times when you may have to fight or run. For me, this was one of those times. I realized I could either fight my fear or cower in fear. I decided to face and fight my fear. By fighting and overcoming my fear with grace, I became a better person; I turned that loss into a win!

Have I totally conquered the fear of public speaking? To be honest, I still get nervous when I stand up in front of a new audience. The difference now? I look on the experience as a chance to grow. I saw it as a chance to expand my comfort zone. I then take a deep breath, step up to the lectern and start to speak.

What's in it for Me?

This chapter is all about learning from your life experiences. I firmly believe that reflecting on your experiences will allow you to learn from those experiences. Learning from your experiences allows you to grow and that growth will allow you to live a happier and more satisfying life. Adapting the habit of reflecting on and learning from both triumphs and setbacks will also allow you to handle (apparent) failure with grace and dignity.

In this chapter I have attempted to provide some insight into learning by sharing some of my personal experiences. Believe

*TURNING LIFE EXPERIENCES INTO
LEARNING EXPERIENCES*

me, some of these were a bit difficult for me to recount. To recap:

1. I learned the importance of the journey through life from a racecar that failed to start.

2. I learned about perseverance during a rather painful first year of teaching.

3. I learned about the joy of helping from the neighborhood kids who helped me move a load of dirt.

4. I learned how to expand my comfort zone by becoming an actor.

I have learned many other life lessons over the years; I selected these because they spanned much of my life. They also illustrated how to learn from, and overcome, experiences that initially appear to be failures.

I also learned a valuable lesson: when you need help, seek help. Don't feel like you need to go it alone. Find a mentor; join a group with similar interests. If you decide to do nothing, you will gain nothing. In fact, you are likely to lose heavily in life, ending up more afraid than before.

SPOTLIGHT ON THE ART OF GRACE

Once you have found someone to help you, be open to their criticism and use their feedback to help you move forward. Work to make progress, but be ready to accept and learn from life's setbacks. That's the trick of "Turning Life Experiences into Life Lessons!"

Discussion Questions

1. Describe an experience of yours that really impacted you either negatively or positively.
2. Did you react gracefully to this experience?
3. Did this experience have a positive or negative impact on you or your family?
4. How has your perspective been changed as a result of this experience?
5. How has this experience changed you?
6. How would your life look differently if you hadn't had the experience?
7. What lesson did you learn from this experience?
8. How has applying this lesson impacted your life?
9. What lesson can you share from this experience?

Biographies

Mark Fegan

Mr. Mark Fegan is a 1975 graduate of Morningside College in Sioux City, Iowa. His primary area of study was Mathematics Education. After graduation Mr. Fegan began a teaching career that lasted twenty years. After starting his career as a Junior High teacher in Minnesota, he taught High School Mathematics in Nebraska and completed this phase of his life in 1996 as an Assistant Professor at Peru State College in Nebraska. Along the way he took a one-year hiatus to work in the garment industry and an additional year off for graduate school. Mr. Fegan earned his MS Ed from Kearney State College in Nebraska in 1979. In 1996, Mr. Fegan changed his focus from teaching to become a Software Developer for Raytheon.

Mr. Fegan joined Toastmasters International in October 2009 and earned Distinguished Toastmaster status in August 2014. Mr. Fegan lives with his wife, Rebecca, in Bellevue, Nebraska, and continues to take an interest in education and helping others achieve their goals.

Contact Mr. Fegan at: mark@alterntivebookclub.com.

Rebecca Fegan

Mrs. Rebecca Fegan, teacher, financial advisor, member of John Maxwell Team, Toastmaster, Lifelong Girl Scout, writer, reader, expert on crutches, mother of 5, grandmother of 4, and all around nice, if weird, person began life in Los Angeles. As

SPOTLIGHT ON THE ART OF GRACE

the daughter of two music teachers, she has developed a rather unique point of view of the world, and a sense of humor that takes some by surprise. After graduating from Illinois State with a degree in Music Education, she went on to get another degree from Peru State College in Business Administration, and then got certifications in life insurance, health insurance, and debt handling, and a Series 65 license in securities. Her favorite authors are John Maxwell and Terry Pratchett, but she also enjoys crime procedural television shows and super hero movies. She is endlessly curious about everything and especially loves cultural geography and travel. Her goal is to make sure that there is a story for every point, for everything to be learned, for every philosophy, and she will go out of her way to collect those stories, including battling vicious revolving doors…

Contact Mrs. Fegan at: rebecca@alternativebookclub.com.

Gloria Harmon

Born and raised in Omaha, Nebraska, Mrs. Gloria Harmon was one of five children. She enlisted in the Women's Army Corp in 1965 and was honorably discharged in 1968. In 1973, she married and had two daughters. At age forty, she went to the University of Nebraska where she received both a Bachelor's of Science and a Master's in education. Mrs. Harmon taught in the Omaha Public Schools until her retirement three years ago. She is always taking classes for self-improvement

Gloria attends Ambassador Worship Center under the leadership of Dr. Martin Williams, a world-renowned teacher, author, speaker and mentor. Several scriptures that she confesses daily are, Galatians 3:29 KJV "And if ye be Christ's, then are ye Abraham's seed and heirs according to the promise." Also, 2 Corinthians 5: 18-19 KJV "And all things are of God, who has reconciled us to himself by Jesus Christ, and hath given to us the ministry of reconciliation; To wit, that God, was in Christ, reconciling the world unto himself, not imputing their trespasses unto them; and hath committed unto us the word of reconciliation." It is with this charge from 2 Corinthians 5:18-19 KJV, that Mrs. Harmon humbly submits the chapter that talks about taking no offense, forgiveness, and humility.

Contact Mrs. Harmon at: gloria@alternativebookclub.com.

George Hast

Mr. Hast was born in Worcester, Massachusetts and is a graduate of Worcester University and a U.S. Navy Veteran. After graduation, he worked for Digital Equipment and later in the small business center at Fleet Bank. In 2001 his wife's father got sick so he moved from the suburbs of Boston to an Iowa cornfield to take care of her father. He worked in credit card fraud detection at First Data. George retired early to care for his ailing wife. He spends his time bicycling around Lake Manawa and watching his beloved Red Sox on TV and

SPOTLIGHT ON THE ART OF GRACE

speaking at Toastmasters International and other groups such as Optimist clubs and the Urban League of Omaha.

Contact Mr. Hast at: george@alternativebookclub.com.

Christine Jones

Mrs. Christine Jones has been spending her days lately learning to be less of an introvert. In order to learn new skills and work on overcoming her fears, she took on the challenge of being Editor for this project. She has been able to experience grace from this group as she went through a surgery and recovery as she worked through this book project. Her life experiences are shared in her chapter, Breaking the Mold. Having been married for over 37 years, to Mr. Keith Jones, and raised two children to successful adults, she has seen first hand how making changes in our "mold" are worth our time and effort. Yes, Mr. Jones, who is also a contributor to this book, is her husband. Working on this together has been an opportunity for her to practice giving him grace in those moments that he felt his words would not come. It was the least she could do after all of his loving support he has given to her through the years!

Yes, she had to practice the skills she discusses in her chapter as she encountered moments of being unsure that she could complete the project. Each time she made the choice to continue and conquer her fears. Doing this as a team allowed her to use others in the group as sounding boards when she was unsure. Read her chapter to learn how she has become less introverted.

Contact Mrs. Jones at: christine@alternativebookclub.com.

Keith Jones

Mr. Keith Jones, born and raised in Cambridge, Nebraska went to college at Kearney State College. He graduated in three straight years with a double major in Computer Science and Mathematics. College is where he met Christine, his wife. He has worked at a construction company, a steel company, a bank, and the local power company. His job duties involved installing operating systems, systems software, and working with the hardware in computer rooms.

Keith and Christine's two children have kept them both busy over the past 27 years. Band, Boy Scouts, and sports provide a wealth of stories and memories for all of us. Trips to Orlando with the high school band, adventures at two Boy Scout National Jamborees, and two trips to Europe with the college band are highlights.

Keith also collects kites that he enjoys flying in his spare time.

Keith has been a member of Toastmasters International for over 28 years. He has a passion for speech contests.

Contact Mr. Jones at: keith@alternativebookclub.com.

SPOTLIGHT ON THE ART OF GRACE

Charles "Chip" Mackenzie

Dr. Chip Mackenzie had polio when he was 6 years old. He went on to get a B.S. in Chemistry from the University of the Pacific and a Ph.D. in Biochemistry from the University of Southern California. He has been divorced, widowed and, is now in his third marriage. He has dealt with the Late Effects of Polio for the last 35 years and is now in a power wheelchair, which he likes to call his 6-wheel ATV. He was nearly 50 years old before he became aware of how often grace had intercepted his life.

Contact Dr. Mackenzie at: chip@alternativebookclub.com.

Evelyn Mosley

Mrs. Evelyn Mosley was born 2 months premature in Omaha, Nebraska to Gloria Jones. She raised Mrs. Mosley and her two younger siblings, Debra and Anthony, as a single parent. Mrs. Mosley was raised in Chicago, Illinois until the age of 8 years. Her family relocated to Omaha where her mother's parents, the late Raymond and Lena, resided. She is the mother of 1 adult son, deceased, and an adult daughter. She is also the grandmother of 8 and the great grandmother of one. One niece calls her Aunt. Mrs. Mosley has been married to Mr. David Mosley for 14 years. The couple has no children together. She finds it an honor and a privilege to be part of this great project of leadership flanked by grace and servitude.

Leading from behind is something that Mrs. Mosley believes all great leaders should adopt. It shows respect, confidence, gratitude, servitude, and, most importantly, it exemplifies grace.

Contact Mrs. Mosley at: evelyn@alternativebookclub.com.

Nick Wolff

Mr. Nick Wolff is a full time consultant, entrepreneur, and educator. He has a wide educational skill set with Master's Degrees in Organizational Development, Business Administration and, Civil Engineering. He is also a candidate for the Doctor of Human Capital Management from Bellevue University. For 15 years, Mr. Wolff worked in the engineering and construction field and served in a management role for over 6 years. During that time, he also provided organizational development and business management consulting services to several organizations, most notably at Motorola and a refinery under the umbrella of a major petrochemical company. In 2013, he founded his own organizational development, education and, business consulting firm. He has worked with Bellevue

SPOTLIGHT ON THE ART OF GRACE

University as an Adjunct Professor in the College of Business and as Program Director of the Master of Industrial and Organizational Psychology and Bachelor of Web Design and Development programs. Mr. Wolff previously published *The Influencer: 107 Lessons on Being Effective without Being a Jerk.*

In his free time, Mr. Wolff speaks professionally, develops educational videos, provides business and leadership development education, and writes educational articles and books. He also spends time with his lively wife, son and, daughters at his home in Omaha, Nebraska.

Contact Mr. Wolff at: nick@alternativebookclub.com.